ANDREW MCHATTIE

ON

COVERED WARRANTS

HARRIMAN HOUSE LTD

43 Chapel Street
Petersfield
Hampshire
GU32 3DY
GREAT BRITAIN

Tel: +44 (0)1730 233870
Fax: +44 (0)1730 233880
email: enquiries@global-investor.com
web site: www.global-investor.com

First published in Great Britain in 2002

Copyright Harriman House Ltd

The right of Andrew McHattie to be identified as the author has been asserted
in accordance with the Copyright, Design and Patents Act 1988.

ISBN 1 897 59720 7

British Library Cataloguing in Publication Data
A CIP catalogue record for this book can be obtained from the British Library.

Printed and bound by Ashford Colour Press Ltd, Gosport, Hampshire.

To Sarah

Biography

Andrew McHattie (MA Cantab) runs the investment publishing company, The McHattie Group. He has been the publisher and editor of the Warrants Alert newsletter since 1989, and edits a range of other warrant publications and services including Warrants Alert Professional, The Warrants Directory, Warrants Magazine, and Warrants Daily. He also publishes the Investment Trust Newsletter and has written for a number of investment magazines. He is a regular speaker on the subjects of warrants and investment trusts. He is chairman of McHattie  Investment Management Limited, which manages an authorised UK unit trust investing in warrants. His previous works on warrants include the best-selling Investor's Guide to Warrants.

Acknowledgements

I have a number of people to thank. My wife Sarah shouldered other responsibilities to make time for me to research and write this book. Others have been generous with their time and help, including Benjamin Cooper, Claire Ever, Philip Jenks, Stephen Eckett, Myles Hunt, Suzanne Anderson, David Lake, Charles Annandale, and Mark Valentine. Pascoe Gibbons deserves a special mention for supplying comprehensive performance data for all covered warrants on Continental European markets.

In undertaking the research for this book I have drawn on the excellent guides produced by issuers, exchanges, and other market participants in established markets around the globe. Much of the material is intelligently and clearly written and has undoubtedly contributed to the success and popularity of these markets.

Contents

Disadvantages

Complexity
Adverse Price Movements
Premium
Limited Life
Time Value Decay
Absence of Price Anomalies
No Income
Scope Still Limited
No Benefit to, or Direct Link with, Companies
No Shareholders' Rights
Need to Have Internet Access
Capital Gains Tax
Credit Risk

Fundamental Analysis
Chart Analysis
Homework – Prices and Terms
Gearing
Intrinsic Value
Premium
Break-Even Point
Capital Fulcrum Point

Black-Scholes
Volatility
- Historical Volatility
- Implied Volatility
- Combining Historical Volatility and Implied Volatility
- Volatility Smile
- Volatility Pyramid
The Greeks
- Delta
- Gamma
- Rho
- Theta
- Vega
- Using the Greeks
Leverage
Concluding Remarks

Introduction

There's a new kid on the block.

Writing in the summer of 2002, the traditional company and investment trust warrants market seems sure to be eclipsed shortly in the UK by a new market which should offer huge opportunities for active investors. Revised regulations have paved the way for a new 'covered warrants' market in London. The number of warrants available to be easily traded by private investors on the London Stock Exchange (LSE) should multiply many times over. Warrants will become available on a broad range of blue-chip companies, sector baskets, and on both UK and overseas indices. You will be able to buy calls and puts. Dealing should be trouble-free in small or large size, and to cap it all the vast majority of the new warrants will be exercisable for cash which will mean they can be traded free of stamp duty. It all sounds very promising.

Whilst new ground is being broken in the UK, the market is following a path well trod by other countries. And unless Australian, Belgian, Dutch, Finnish, French, German, Hong Kong, Italian, Japanese, Portugese, South African, Swedish, and Swiss investors are all differently motivated from British investors, the market has a very strong chance of success. It will need to attract a new constituency of investors though, since very few investors have traded warrants actively in the UK in the past. It may take a little while for the educational process to filter through to dealing volumes. And recent bearish market conditions have hardly helped the appetite for geared instruments which amplify price movements. The recent poor performance of traditional listed warrants has left a legacy of doubt and suspicion. There is little residue of goodwill. This means that advocates of the new covered warrants market will have to work hard to win over new investors. The good news is that the advocates are numerous and armed with some potent remedies for ailing portfolios.

There is a good reason why the more colourful exponents of the market use words like turbo, supercharged, race-tuned, supersonic and jet-propelled. There is a good reason why warrant brochures are jammed with pictures of racing cars, rockets, jet aircraft, roller-coasters, express trains, cheetahs, and bullets. Warrants are the speed merchants of the stockmarket. Equity warrants can produce tremendous gains in bullish market conditions, and covered warrants go one step better. They offer the thrill of big profits in all weathers. Examples are not hard to find from overseas markets of large profits which have been made from underlying asset movements in either direction, and some of the gains are simply mouth-watering, such as the Commerzbank Euro/US Dollar 09/02 0.95 currency call warrants which have translated a 13% increase in the euro over the last three months into a huge profit of 933% on the warrants; or the Goldman Sachs S&P500 09/02 1000 put warrants which converted a 27% drop in the market over three months into a 784% gain for the warrants; or the BNP Paribas Deutsche Telekom 03/03 20 call warrants which have risen by 467% in response to an 18% rise in the share price over just one month; or the SG Oracle 09/02 18 call warrants which are up by 115% after an 11% share price rise over the month; or the JPMorgan Alitalia 09/02 0.703 put warrants which have flown up by 205% after the shares dropped by 24% over the month. The list goes on, and for smart investors able to select the right warrants there are always some rich pickings to be had. In one French guide to covered warrants the words "significativement enrichi" hold a prominent place, the meaning of which is evident without language skills.

The premier attraction of warrants has always been their ability to produce large gains from small market movements, yet few investors appreciate the wide range of applications for which warrants are suitable. Even if market conditions are unhelpful they can be used in other ways to produce profits or to cut losses.

This book is intended as a primer for investors new to covered warrants, although more experienced investors may also find some value in the timely information about the formation of the new market in London. Readers used to dealing in traditional listed warrants in the UK will find the new covered warrants quite different. Jargon is unavoidable, but it is explained in the text and in the glossary at the back. You may like to dip into the book as your needs and interests determine, but it is designed to be read sequentially.

- Chapter 1 guides you through each element of what covered warrants are, step-by-step.

- A quick trip around the world in Chapter 2 to assess their global importance then brings us back to the UK.

- Chapters 3 and 4 deal with the decline of traditional warrants in the UK and the development of the new covered warrants market. The next section is concerned with practical matters.

- Chapter 5 considers the different varieties of covered warrants and their terms.

• Chapter 6 provides detailed information on pricing and trading.

• Once you know what covered warrants are, why they have been issued, and precisely how you can deal, Chapter 7 weighs their advantages and disadvantages. If you are persuaded of the merits of covered warrants, it is then time to move from the general to the specific.

• Chapters 8 and 9 deal with the analysis and selection of warrants.

• Having chosen your warrants, you may be ready to plunge in, but not before Chapter 10's reminder about risk, which must not be overlooked.

• Chapter 11 suggests differing approaches to trading and investment.

• Finally, Chapter 12 concludes with a look ahead to the future and some indications of how the market may develop.

Certainly one of the key changes for British warrant investors is that information will become much more readily available. For years there has been only one general book on warrants, one newsletter, just a couple of introductory guides, and few, if any, seminars. That will all change. The London Stock Exchange, the banks who issue covered warrants, and stockbrokers executing the deals are all anxious to make this new market a roaring success, and for it to work they need investors to understand the market, trade skilfully, and prosper. To this end an abundance of guides, on-line tutorials, seminars, and other educational material will be made available, and much of it free of charge. Investors have a wonderful new opportunity to learn about warrants, and if this book helps in a small way then it will have served its purpose. The key to all successful investment is to be properly informed, and there is no reason why any intelligent investor should not attain a first-class understanding of covered warrants. Long price codes, tables of ratios prefaced by Greek letters, and muttered references to such esoterica as deltas, leverage, implied volatility, and barriers are bound to be confusing when taken as a whole, but they are not difficult to understand when explained singly and simply.

In any event, the effort required to learn about warrants is a worthwhile investment. At the very least you might otherwise wonder what all the fuss is about as this market develops and begins to receive much more coverage in the press. The introduction of covered warrants for private investors is easi-ly the most significant revolution in the UK warrants market for decades. And once the market is up and running and investors can see for themselves how it works, the returns which are possible may well start to make headlines. The fear that warrants are too complicated is largely a fear of the unknown, and once observation begins to strip away the mystery there is a good chance that greed and curiosity will take over from trepidation and ignorance. And of course profits are the best salesmen of all.

Out of necessity the examples used in this book are from overseas covered warrant markets, because the UK market is not yet underway at the time of writing. There are some regional differences in the structure of warrants and in some terminology, and of course in local governing rules, but all covered warrants markets have much in common, and the comparisons are valid. Do be aware, however, that the UK market may develop quickly, and perhaps deviate from its initial blueprint, which places an onus on you to check any important features which may have a bearing on your investment plan.

1. What is a Covered Warrant?

Definition and Basic Attributes

So let's start at the very beginning. What is a covered warrant? Here is a definition from the London Stock Exchange, taken from its Covered Warrant Market Service Description, 2002:

> A covered warrant is a proprietary instrument, issued by a financial institution, that bestows on the holder the right, but not an obligation, to buy or sell an asset at a specified strike price during, or at the end of, a specified time period. Covered warrants may be either 'calls' or 'puts', where a call warrant is analogous to a long position in the underlying and a put warrant is analogous to a short position in the underlying. In terms of contract styles, covered warrants can be European or American style. The former means that the warrant can be exercised only at expiration, whilst in the latter case this can be at any time up to expiry. The holder can exercise the instrument for cash or shares, depending on the prospectus of the issuer. The gearing inherent in covered warrants means that the purchase price is typically less than the price of the underlying on which the warrant is based. As holders will always have a 'long' position, be it with calls or puts, the maximum loss is confined to the premium paid, and the exercise is always against the issuer of the covered warrant. Unlike company warrants, covered warrants do not create new shares in issue.

It may be better to treat the process of warrant definition as a glass of fine wine. Swallowing the whole lot in one great gulp can make you dizzy. It is better to sip. There is a lot to savour. Not only are warrants composed of a number of elements, but those elements vary markedly between differing forms of warrants, of which there is a broad array. And just as different wines are suitable for different drinkers, different tables, and different budgets, covered warrants offer equal diversity. There are call warrants and put warrants, American-style warrants and European-style warrants, vanilla warrants and exotic warrants, stock warrants and index warrants, instalment warrants and basket warrants, currency warrants and commodity warrants, in-the-money and out-of-the-money warrants, cash-settled and stock-settled warrants. The word 'warrant' refers generally to a form of authorisation –

hence its common legal usage - and it has been hijacked by financial engineers as a sweeping term to represent a class of structured products which provide some form of right to invest.

More simply, then, a warrant is a right to buy or sell an asset at a fixed price, on or before a specified future date. Warrants are similar to options. They present opportunities for capital gains which make them an attractive medium for speculative investing, although they can be used to serve a variety of aims. You can buy and sell covered warrants at any time during their defined life.

Covered warrants are securities issued by banks or financial institutions. They are synthetic financial products which are created to meet the investment requirements of individuals, and occasionally, institutions. They may give rights over a single share, or a group of shares, an index, a currency, a commodity, or almost any other financial asset. The common theme is that they enable investors to obtain exposure to the performance of the asset for a fraction of the price. This is called gearing. Instead of paying 100p for a share, warrants might provide the same profit potential for 20p, and this lower price means that their percentage gains (or losses) are greater. Gearing means that you get more bang for your buck. Or to put it another way, and to pinch a phrase from a new Commerzbank guide to the market, warrants are a way to make your money work harder.

This does not explain why they are called covered warrants. The name was coined when these forms of warrants were first created, when they generally held rights to purchase a physical stock at the end of their term. Each warrant was therefore covered by the underlying security, which was held by the issuer in order to satisfy the exercise right when the warrants reached maturity. Now very few warrants are ever exercised for stock, and the issuer instead seeks to cover the financial exposure adopted when issuing a warrant by undertaking some matching financial transactions, using dynamic hedging techniques, sometimes with the stock itself but more frequently with other derivatives such as futures and options. Issuers of warrants are to some degree acting as intermediaries to repackage the financial exposure into a listed security.

According to the Financial Services Authority (FSA), the regulatory body overseeing UK financial products, covered warrants are a class of securitised derivative. Simply, these are derivatives that are freely traded and are listed on stock exchanges. Covered warrants are the most prominent type of securitised derivative, but this broader term also encompasses products such as certificates with guaranteed return elements. These products work in the following way: the investor pays an amount of money up front in return for a right to receive a return, either in cash or by the physical delivery of some underlying instrument. They allow more sophisticated investors to have access to a wide range of underlying products without having to invest directly in them.

There was a considerable degree of reluctance from the fledgling warrants fraternity in the UK to calling covered warrants securitised derivatives, because derivatives are commonly thought of as being dangerous, devious, devilish instruments which can destabilise markets and quickly become ruinous in experienced hands. The 'd-word' has some negative connotations. This is true, and classifying covered warrants as pure derivatives would have been a quick route to a dead-end in marketing terms. Securitised derivatives is a more workable concept, although it might still need some explaining to a sceptical public entirely unfamiliar with the term.

Comparison between Corporate Warrants and Covered Warrants

There are several key differences between covered warrants and traditional listed equity, or corporate, warrants, with which British investors are slightly more familiar. Even those investors most familiar and conversant with the workings, analysis and selection of UK equity warrants will probably find huge gaps in their knowledge when the time comes - as it surely will - to consider covered warrants.

There is a lot to learn, some of which is common sense, and some of which is more appropriate for mathematically-inclined readers who find the whole process of analysis and selection absorbing. The process of issuance is different, and the way in which prices are formed is different, which in turn means that traditional forms of analysis need to be adapted and developed. It will not be sufficient to stick with the same valuation models, applying them directly to the new covered warrants. Using a flat screwdriver to turn a Phillips screw works up to a point, but it lacks force at the point of tension - when you really need it to work.

Having the right tools for the job means understanding where important characteristics differ between traditional listed equity warrants and covered warrants. The key differences are set out in the table overleaf.

Traditional listed equity warrants	Covered warrants
Issued by company over its own shares	Issued by bank or institution over other assets
New shares issued upon exercise	No new shares issued
Call warrants only	Call, put, and exotic warrant structures
Maturities typically several years	Maturities typically one or two years
Restricted liquidity	Good liquidity
Held by individuals and by institutions	Designed for private investors
Priced according to supply and demand	Priced according to fair value models
Price competition among market-makers	Price competition from different warrant issues
Data and information scarce	Data and information readily available
Stamp duty payable	Stamp duty not payable if cash-settled
Must sign risk warning notice before dealing	No need to sign risk warning notice
Listed on the London Stock Exchange	Listed on the London Stock Exchange

Some elements are different, and some are the same. The various aspects are explained at greater length throughout this book, but the point to note for now is that there are significant differences between the two forms of warrants. On occasions covered warrants have been described as an evolution of traditional warrants, but this implies they are refined and improved versions, whereas in practice they have their rough edges too. Covered warrants cannot offer a perfect way for everyone to invest and speculate. What they can offer is an extra dimension to flat portfolios, a pick-me-up for tired assets, an element of spice to the most insipid investments, a high risk and reward challenge for hands-on investors striving to build their wealth.

2. Overseas Markets

If covered warrants are such a grand idea, able to produce fabulous returns, why have they not been available before now? The answer is that they have – outside the UK. British regulators have been slow to catch on and catch up, and whilst institutional investors have been able to invest in covered warrants in London for years, private investors have endured the frustration of seeing the concept developed fully in a wide range of other markets, led by the major bourses of Europe.

The growth of international covered warrant markets has been astonishing. According to the International Warrant Institute the total number of warrants issued globally at 30th June 2001 was just under 48,000, compared with 36,000 six months earlier. By the end of 2001 this number had risen again to 53,608. This frenetic pace of issuance has been driven partly by burgeoning demand from investors, and partly by the need for issuers to continually realign their product range to adapt to changing underlying stocks and markets.

The most warrants, by far, have been issued in Germany, with over 24,000 issues at present, with Italy growing strongly in second place, boasting nearly 6,000 warrants. The largest issuers globally have been Citibank, Société Générale (SG), Goldman Sachs, UBS, BNP Paribas, Commerzbank, Unicredito, Credit Lyonnais, Dresdner Bank, and Lehman Brothers. As far as choice is concerned, any investor wanting warrant exposure to, say, Nokia, has a wide selection from which to choose. The Institute's data found no fewer than 649 warrants available on Nokia – or more than five times the total number of equity warrants currently in issue on all companies on the UK listed market.

More up to date figures from Société Générale show that in May 2002, £1bn of covered warrants were traded in Switzerland alone, followed by Italy and Hong Kong. Germany came fourth by volume, followed by France, Australia, South Africa, Spain, Finland, and Portugal. Overall, some £4bn of warrants were traded globally during the month - consistent with data from Goldman Sachs showing that £52bn of covered warrants were traded in 2001.

Anyone who doubts whether covered warrants will take off in the UK should just look at the experience of other markets. Even if the market is not an instant hit, investors should soon realise the benefits of warrants trading – particularly if market conditions are benign and those who try it start to make some huge profits. There are too many global success stories to run through all markets comprehensively, but a quick tour is useful for demonstrating how positively investors have received this product elsewhere.

Germany

Covered warrant markets are certainly well established in Europe. The Swiss market started in 1986, followed by Germany in 1989, and premium turnover exceeded EU50bn on the Continent in 2001. In Germany, now the largest covered warrants market in the world, there are on average 15,000 trades every day in covered warrants, with the average deal size around EU10,000. More than 90% of trades come from private investors.

There are actually four stock exchanges in Germany which offer warrant trading, and a lot of trading is also conducted directly with the issuers off-exchange, but one exchange stands out with a large market share. EUWAX® - the European Warrant Exchange - was created by the Stuttgart Stock Exchange in July 1999 as a special market segment for warrants, certificates, and other securitised derivatives. In June 2002 a total of 30 issuers (including all of those proposing to issue in London) had listed 22,463 warrants, making this the largest exchange-traded warrants market in the world. The majority of warrants (71%) have equities as the underlying asset. Index warrants weigh in with 17%, and currency warrants account for 9%. On a busy day there can be 200 new warrants issued. The UK is unlikely to reach this kind of level for some time. Indeed, the need to avoid placing the new systems under too much stress will mean that some limits are placed on the issuers initially so that the market starts off at a relatively gentle pace. Even so, the dramatic growth of covered warrants in Germany gives London something to aim at.

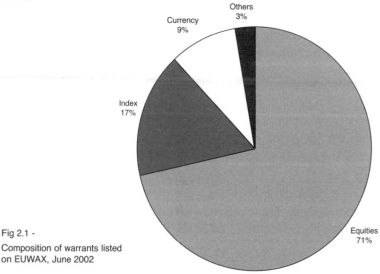

Fig 2.1 -
Composition of warrants listed
on EUWAX, June 2002

EUWAX attributes its success to a number of guiding principles which lay emphasis on providing a service to investors which they will want to use. It is no coincidence that they start with:

• maximum investor protection by way of strict trading controls (the foundation for any successful derivative market where the risk profile means the stakes are high)

• transparency of the trading process

• fair execution of orders guaranteed by the regulatory & technical framework

• concentration of liquidity on a single platform, guaranteeing executions at the prevailing market prices

• quick execution of orders

• ability of investors to reconcile their orders and the transacted prices

• comprehensive information and top-quality service for investors

• the establishment of an internationally recognised trading platform

• a high-quality learning system, called IceLearning

Most of these factors, with the possible exception of the last, should also apply to the new London market.

The most actively traded warrants on EUWAX by far are warrants on the domestic Xetra DAX Index of leading shares. Investors also use covered warrants to take positions on other global indices such as the S&P 500, the Dow Jones, and the DJ Euro Stoxx 50. Single-stock warrants on German companies such as Deutsche Telekom and Allianz also tend to be popular.

The large overall number of warrants in issue, and the wide availability of both calls and puts means that a day does not pass without some massive gains and losses being recorded (usually called the tops and flops, or toppers and floppers). On one day at the time of writing, for example, the top 20 warrant performers on the EUWAX all posted gains of 1200% or more. Those were the gains on the day. At the top was a Euro/Yen currency warrant which moved up from EU0.024 to EU5.44 over the day for a gain of 22,566%. Of course, the same pattern of extreme results is repeated on the downside, and the worst 20 performers over the day all posted losses in excess of 93%. The worst was a DAX Knock-Out warrant with a scheduled maturity of another month but which hit its barrier level of 3600 as the index plunged 4.8% to 3515, causing the warrant to immediately expire worthless. In a large market with a good range and choice of warrants, the twin features of risk and reward are omnipresent for all to see.

Italy

Here are some facts about the Italian market.

- The Borsa Italiana had 5786 covered warrants at the end of June 2002.

- In the same month, the trading turnover in warrants was a shade over EU2bn from 482,000 trades. That's around 25,000 trades per day.

- In the first 6 months of the year turnover was EU10.9bn from 3.09m trades.

- There are 25 active issuers. Unicredito Italiano is slightly ahead of Société Générale by number and by turnover: both have over 900 warrants in issue.

- Nearly all of the warrants, 5505, are plain vanilla, and about 75% are calls.

- Nearly 4000 warrants are available on domestic shares, and over 1000 on various market indices.

- By far the most popular are those on the MIB 30 Italian stockmarket index. The Nasdaq 100 is also a very popular underlying asset, as are leading Italian companies such as ENI, TIM, Telecom Italia, Generali, and Olivetti.

- The Borsa's electronic trading platform for warrants, introduced in July 2000, has capacity for 10,000 listings and 3m trading orders per day.

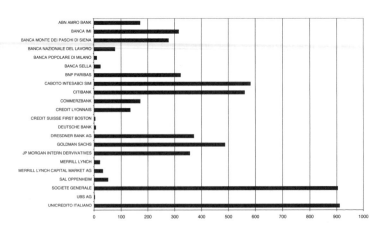

Fig 2.2 - Covered warrants by issuer, Borsa Italiana, June 2002

The message is clear. Covered warrants are very popular in Italy, and the market is well served by a large number of issuers creating a broad range of warrants. Yet the market is young: it started in the second half of 1998, since when "the growth rate has been impressive" the exchange says modestly. The sector boomed when lower interest rates led Italian investors to look at equities, and covered warrants caught their imagination. The growth of online trading helped too, as investors used the internet to source information and data before dealing using their computers.

Euronext

British investors may not be familiar with Euronext, but it is a major force in European equity markets. It is an amalgamation of the Paris, Amsterdam, Brussels and Lisbon markets which have combined to enable faster and more cost-effective trading. It bought the London International Financial Futures Exchange (LIFFE) in 2001 for £555m.

The market has a special NextWarrants® segment for buying and selling warrants. This automated trading platform is the home for around 6000 warrants, providing investment access to assets around the world. A 'liquidity provider', usually the issuer, is obliged to enter quotes throughout trading sessions and to maintain a minimum size and maximum spread. The idea is to create a liquid and attractive market place. It is also comparatively quick and easy for issuers to list new warrants – listings can usually be achieved within seven days. The admission fee is EU1000 per warrant plus EU500 per warrant per year to maturity, plus some other fees for checking prospectuses and the like.

Some may find it difficult to swallow the fact that London has been beaten to the punch by Lisbon. Portugal is not usually regarded as a first-rank global equity market, but it has

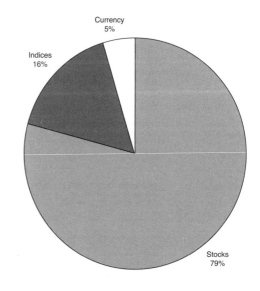

Fig 2.3 - Composition of French warrants by sector, July 2002

enjoyed a growing warrant market since 2000 when EU123m of warrants were traded, rising to EU684m in 2001. Some regulatory amendments in 2001 broadened the scope to allow the issue of basket warrants. By the end of 2001 some 321 warrants were listed with a market capitalisation of EU3587m. Data from Commerzbank for mid-July 2002 showed that the number was roughly the same, with a total of 312 warrants listed at this time. There were slightly more in both the Netherlands (469), and Belgium (520). The majority of Euronext warrants belong to the French market, which had 5474 warrants listed in mid-July 2002 according to the French company Oddo & Cie, with the great bulk of these (79%) in single stock warrants.

Switzerland

The covered warrants market in Switzerland is the oldest and one of the most active. There were 4070 warrants listed at the end of 2001, up from 2449 a year earlier and just 1087 in 1999. About 15% of the warrants were on market indices, but most trade was in individual stock warrants, with Swiss companies to the fore. Warrants on ABB, Zurich Finance, Credit Suisse, Novartis, Nestlé, UBS, Roche, Swiss Re, and Swisscom were the most numerous.

Originally, covered warrants were issued in Switzerland to provide access to equities where individual shares were priced too highly for private investors to buy. Lower-priced warrants could be bought even if the underlying shares were out of reach. This is less of an issue today, but covered warrants have retained their popularity.

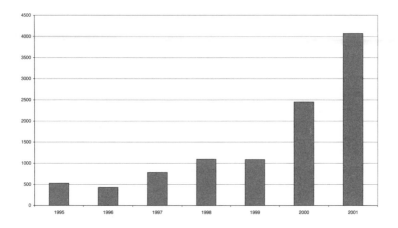

Fig 2.4 - Number of warrants listed in Switzerland, 1995-2001

Spain

In Spain, the term 'retail investor' has been taken literally - the issuer SG has actually opened a shop in Madrid to supply investors with a range of services relevant to warrant trading, including access to a library, courses and conferences, screens displaying live prices, and, apparently, a well-stocked bar. Market participants have had cause to raise a glass or two as the market has grown markedly since its introduction in 1995. Indeed it claims to be the fastest-growing market in the world in percentage terms – a title which could yet be claimed by London if all goes well. The number of new issues started very modestly in Madrid with 11 in 1995 and 13 in 1996 before jumping to 65 in 1997. The number fell to 46 in 1998 before really pushing on as demand grew: 161 in 1999, 332 in 2000, and 851 in 2001. By the end of April 2002 there had already been a further 817 new issues, which, after taking account of some expiries, lifted the overall number of warrants in issue to 1490. The total had slipped slightly to 1257 by mid-July as global markets slid, but this does not detract greatly from the spectacular growth in issues over the past four years. The rise of the market as a significant portion of the Spanish equity market has been accompanied by an increase in the number of issuers. Domestic issuers include Banco Bilbao Vizcaya Argentaria, Santander General Hispano, and Banesto. Overseas issuers include SG, Citibank, UBS Warburg, BNP Paribas, and Commerzbank.

The range of warrants in Spain is broad, with Spanish and foreign shares, indices, interest rates, currencies, commodities, and baskets of securities all covered. Domestic stocks account for 60% of all warrants in issue, with international stocks the next most popular grouping.

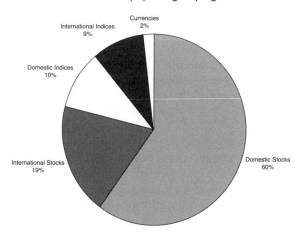

Fig 2.5 - Composition of Spanish warrants by sector, April 2002

Far from resting on its laurels, the Spanish market is making strenuous efforts to improve the market further, and in 2002 introduced a new electronic trading segment to consolidate a market which already enjoys wide acceptance amongst investors.

Scandinavia

Finland's stockmarket is utterly dominated by the mobile telephone company Nokia, which at the end of 2001 accounted for EU137bn of the total market capitalisation of EU217bn on the Helsinki Exchanges. Nokia is a highly visible and highly volatile international stock which has attracted enormous covered warrant issuance on a number of markets – including Helsinki itself. The exchange's interim report for the first quarter of 2002 reported that "the strongest growth was seen in covered warrants, where the trading volume reached EU81m. In the corresponding period of 2001, the figure was EU5m." Trading only began in covered warrants in Helsinki in December 2000, and the first index warrants were launched by SG in July 2001. A total of 112 warrants were in issue at the end of 2001, with 513m warrants traded over the year, a turnover amounting to EU118m.

Sweden is the largest market in the region with nearly 2000 warrants listed on the Stockholm exchange. Warrants on domestic companies such as ABB, Ericsson, Pharmacia, Skandia, Tele2, and Volvo are joined (inevitably) by a large number of warrants on Nokia and on indices such as the Nasdaq 100 and the local OMX index.

Australia

Rugby and cricket fans will be well used to England being beaten by Australia. We might expect to have the edge when it comes to financial markets, but in the field of warrants the Australians have again put us to shame. The London Stock Exchange's new plans come no less than 11 years after a similar market was established in Australia. At first, trading was quiet, and then since 1995 it has grown quickly and become a great success. Even in the recent depressed markets, figures from the Australian Stock Exchange show warrant trades running at over 30,000 per month, or A$320m in value. The number of warrants in issue has grown every year since 1995, to reach nearly 1400 by August 2002. Investors can trade in a wide variety of calls and puts on both companies and indices, international warrants, barrier calls, currency warrants, endowment warrants, and instalment warrants. There are frequent warrant seminars and lecture courses to educate investors.

Warrants are considered an important and integral part of the stockmarket, which is perhaps not the case in the UK at present.

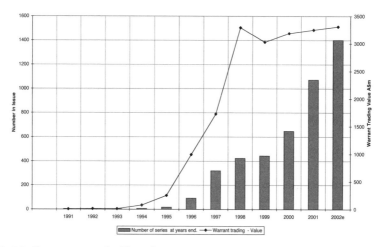

Fig 2.6 - Year on year growth of Australian warrants, 1991-2001

The market is still growing in Australia, and warrants turnover has continued to rise in spite of a general downturn in markets. Warrant volumes increased from 9.04bn in 2000/01 to 11.05bn in 2001/02, a 22% increase. Likewise, the value of trades increased from A$2.34bn in 2000/01 to A$3.21bn in 2001/02 – a 17% rise. Product innovation has helped. The Australian market provides a good example of how covered warrants can be adapted to local needs and react efficiently to local tax laws. A form of security called instalment warrants has become very popular, such that 45% of trades in warrants are currently in these instruments. Like ordinary stock warrants, instalment warrants provide a geared exposure to an underlying share, but they differ in that the share is actually bought and held in trust for investors. These warrants are, in other words, covered by the underlying shares, and they are even structured so that the warrant holder is entitled to the dividends and franking credits. Typically, an instalment warrant might require a 50% down payment, and the issuer effectively lends the remaining 50%, plus interest, some of which is prepaid in the first instalment. These interest expenses may be eligible for tax deductions. Endowment warrants are also issued which are investment products typically with a ten-year life. They allow investors to benefit from companies paying out dividend yields which are higher than prevailing interest rates. Australian issuers have responded to a demand for investment-style warrants rather than speculative warrants, and have been able to introduce very successful modifications to provide long-term exposure with tax benefits.

Hong Kong

Asian private investors are frequently characterised with a gambling mentality, which may or may not be fair, but it comes as no real surprise that there are active covered warrant markets in the Far East. They cannot match the European markets for dealing volumes or for the number of warrants in issue, however, and their development has been far from smooth.

In Hong Kong the market was put to sleep for the second half of 2001 with a moratorium imposed on any new issues pending new regulations. A re-think was needed because the market was expensive for investors, and was not functioning very well. Sure enough, the new regulations announced in December 2001 scrapped the pre-placement regulations which had imposed a minimum warrant size of HK$50m and a requirement that 85% of the issue be pre-placed with at least 100 investors. Unfortunately some parties had begun to circumvent these rules by arranging for connected investors to take up warrants on the understanding that they could later sell them back. This smacked of a 'magic circle' arrangement like that which has come to haunt some split capital investment trust investors in the UK. The high minimum size also made the market uneconomic for some issuers, and the lack of competition generally meant that prices were high.

There is now a looser requirement for a minimum issue size of HK$10m, and issuers no longer need to pre-place warrants, which makes warrant issue programmes far simpler. As a result some new banks have entered the market, and the sector looks at least partly revitalised with the number of new warrants since the re-launch in triple figures.

A continuous market-making system has also improved liquidity for traders, so dealing volumes are beginning to pick up again. According to figures from the largest issuer, KBC Financial, the average daily turnover in covered warrants for the period between 29th January and 9th May 2002 was HK$550m.

That said, there remain drawbacks with the market. With high listing fees, it is expensive to issue warrants in Hong Kong, at a cost of around HK$250,000 to HK$300,000, leading Rupert Rothenhauser, the global head of retail listed products for BNP Paribas to observe "Hong Kong's charge is about four to 23 times higher than its European counterparts." This is why the number of warrants in Hong Kong is measured in hundreds (411 in July 2002) rather than thousands and why the market is far less significant than in most European countries.

Singapore

Although warrants have been traded in the country since late 1997, Singapore provides a rare example of a covered warrant market which has not worked in recent times. Stalling investor demand has met with poor disclosure and comparatively rigid regulations to cap activity at a low level, and industry participants were disappointed with new rules from the SGX exchange which were introduced at the start of July 2002. In particular, the SGX has kept placement rules which require a minimum size of S$5m with at least S$3.75m of that to be placed out to a minimum of 100 warrant holders. This restrictive rule stifles product innovation and issuance, and the absence of a market-making middleman to provide pricing and liquidity is a further problem which prevents the market from prospering.

Already the market has to overcome considerable negative investor psychology after a string of poorly performing call warrants, and the level of education offered to investors has not been sufficient to explain the merits of covered warrants in differing market conditions. Statistical data in particular has not always been readily available, which means that it has been difficult for individuals to assess the valuation of warrants and to calculate what will happen to their warrant holdings under different scenarios. On occasions it has been suggested that investors were hurried to invest in pre-market placings on the basis of inadequate term sheets which omitted key valuation information such as implied volatility. Whether or not this was the case, it seems that investors have not fully understood the investment proposition, which meant they walked away at the first sign of losses.

At the time of writing there are only two remaining covered warrants listed in Singapore, and it seems likely that in the absence of either some new regulations or a powerful bull market, neither of which seem likely in the short-term, the market will remain in a moribund state.

Japan

The Nikkei 225 Index reached its peak at the end of 1989, since when it has been on a downward slide which has driven large numbers of investors well away from equity markets. Financial innovation has been used to try and entice them back again, and covered warrants are amongst a broad range of equity-related products on offer. A deregulation of over-the-counter sales of derivatives in December 1998 led to the introduction of covered warrants, helped further by the deregulation of brokerage commission rates in October 1999. A new online broking market rapidly developed offering customers drastically lower dealing charges. Goldman Sachs began to offer warrants and certificates to investors from March 2000 through direct connections to major online brokers. This business model is in contrast to the exchange driven models common in Europe. Over 800 warrants are available in Japan, forming a sophisticated covered warrant market where the general term is used to cover a spread of instruments, from bond-backed warrants linked to the movement of the yen against the dollar, to covered warrants linked to hedge funds, where 80% of the amount invested in the warrants is guaranteed even if the underlying funds deteriorate.

Goldman Sachs dominates the market in Japan with a 90%-plus share of securitised derivative volumes, but in June 2001 the firm ran into trouble with the Japanese regulators for displaying an incorrect price. A covered warrant on a Japanese banking share was priced on an internet system for about half an hour at a mistaken bid price of ¥204 when it should have been around ¥8. Goldman Sachs received selling orders totalling ¥157m from 28 investors during that time, and later asked clients with erroneous profits to cancel the transactions. The firm was ordered to suspend trading for two weeks, to halt issuing and offering new warrants for a month, and was in addition banned from Japanese government bond auctions for a month. Goldman Sachs called the ruling "harsh and disproportionate", but Iichiro Yoshino, an official for the Japanese Financial Services Agency, said the severe punishment had been appropriate because Goldman Sachs accounted for a high proportion of covered warrant transactions and bore a heavy responsibility for its growth. The regulators ordered the company to improve its information disclosure on covered warrant trading and to introduce measures to prevent such a mistake from happening again. Some commentators felt there may have been a political edge to what on the surface seems a harsh reaction to a data entry error, as distinct from a deliberate breach, but the episode did serve to underline the regulator's fierce determination to ensure the smooth running of the market.

South Africa

Warrants were introduced in South Africa by Deutsche Bank in 1997, since when the Johannesburg Stock Exchange (JSE) says "this market has seen exponential growth." It leapt out of the blocks quickly, with 250m warrants traded during the first seven months, and has accelerated since. During the third quarter of 2001, trade in more than 500 warrants accounted for almost 50% of the total volume on the exchange. Most warrant traders are private individuals. As one would expect, warrants on resource stocks are popular,

with warrants on companies such as Goldfields, Harmony Gold Mining, Richemont Securities, Sasol, Anglogold, and Anglo American Platinum Corporation amongst the most heavily traded.

Canada

Canada joins Singapore as a relative failure in the booming world of warrants, this time largely because market conditions have been extremely unfavourable. Montreal is the home for warrant trading in Canada. The exchange is known for its derivatives, and in January 2002 started trading in what it calls 'sponsored options', or covered warrants.

Citibank and Société Générale were the first two sponsors, but Citibank withdrew from the market in June 2002, leaving SG as the sole issuer with under 100 warrants in issue. The underlying companies for the warrants include Amazon, AOL, Cisco, Dell, Intel, Merck, Microsoft, Nokia, Nortel, Oracle, and Pfizer. The range is small, but the dealing volumes have been nothing short of derisory. The entire number of warrants traded for the first half of 2002 was 223,083, which works out at just over 2000 warrants traded per day. The average daily value of trading was C$918.94, which quickly explains why Citibank decided to withdraw.

Gamely, the Bourse de Montreal says the market is in its early stages of development and that exotic sponsored options might arrive in the next phase of introduction, but volumes will need to pick up markedly if it is to have any future at all. This might happen if markets begin to recover in general terms. Warrants have less of a grip in North America than in Europe, and may face a struggle to establish themselves in Canada.

Why not the US?

So far the largest economy and the largest equity market in the world has not had a mention. In view of the fact that many of the largest global warrants issuers are American banks – Citibank, Goldman Sachs, JPMorgan, and Lehman Brothers – it is ironic that covered warrants do not exist in the US. Options market are extensive and well developed, the regulatory framework is unhelpful, and American investors seeking geared exposure can already use Long-Term Equity Anticipation Securities (LEAPS), which generally have a maturity of three years and are, appropriately enough, American-style options. There seems little prospect of any developments for the US to follow Europe's lead.

Lessons

Drawing together some observations from overseas markets, certain common factors emerge as important if a local covered ▓▓▓▓ ▓▓▓▓ is to be successful. Low charges, flexible regulations, an ▓▓▓▓▓ ▓▓▓▓ and favourable market conditions can all help covered war▓▓▓ ▓▓▓ ▓▓ ▓▓▓ ▓▓▓ flourish they have. With the exceptions of Singapore a▓▓ ▓▓▓▓ ▓▓▓▓▓ warrants have proved popular wherever they have bee▓ ▓▓▓▓ ▓▓▓ ▓▓▓▓ does not seem to have been any widespread problem ▓▓▓ ▓▓▓▓▓▓ understanding or appreciation of the risks.

The one local factor which is really different in the Uk ▓ ▓▓▓ ▓▓▓▓▓▓ of a substantial spread-betting industry which already meets – quite well – the speculative needs of investors with scope to make money from decreases as well as increases in share prices. Spread betting is probably the closest competitor for the new warrants market. The market leader in that sector, IG Index, has more than quintupled its turnover in four years and has increased its client base from 5000 clients in 1998 to 16,000 by 2002 in spite of considerable new competition. Although some of these clients bet on sports rather than financial instruments, there is certainly an existing base of sophisticated individuals already familiar with the process of two-way derivative speculation. IG has an estimated 35% share of the financial market. IG Index itself recognises the close link between spread betting and covered warrants: when it decided in 2002 to expand into Australia, which was its first geographic diversification apart from a small office in Pakistan, it hired a local expert with previous experience in retail covered warrants to run the operation.

The fight will be on for market share between spread betting and covered warrants, and to a lesser extent, Contracts for Differences (CFDs). Even if covered warrants find it more difficult in the UK to capture such a large percentage of speculative investors as elsewhere, they will surely make their mark.

3. History and Development (i)
Out With the Old

In the early 1990s the traditional warrants market was booming in the UK. It looked unstoppable. Issuance was high, the performance was superb, and speculative investors in particular were drawn to the sector. It is not hard to understand why. In 1993 the average warrant more than trebled in value, and some profits were simply stratospheric. The top-performing warrants in that year belonged to Sphere Investment Trust: the price rocketed from 0.5p to 9p. JF Philippine Fund warrants soared from 18.5p to 304p. Turkey Trust warrants strutted from 18p to 193p. Even those investors who opted for more conservative warrants did well: no less than 70% of all warrants doubled over the year, and only two fell in value. It is little wonder then that the market exerted a magnetic pull for speculators and investors alike.

From Boom to Bust in a Decade

Soon though the smooth progress of the market ran into trouble. Many of the investment trusts which had rushed to issue warrants in the boom of 1993 and 1994 were linked either to emerging markets or to Japan, both of which began to perform poorly. Emerging markets were hit by currency crises, and Japan fell into recession. These two sectors dragged the market down shortly after many new private investors had first discovered warrants, meaning that for many their first experiences involved some heavy losses. Not surprisingly, they were unimpressed, and found the gearing of warrants hard to stomach when it worked in reverse. Warrants fell by 20% in 1994, 14% in 1995, and 12% in 1996. As quickly as they came, investors deserted the warrants market in droves, exacerbating the price falls and reducing market liquidity, making it more difficult for the remaining participants to deal actively.

Limited Issuance and Liquidity

A dark cloud of negative sentiment was seeded by gloomy investors, and the investment trust industry which had used warrants so freely in the 1990s to plug the discount gap for new launches, had a change of heart. Beset first by demands from institutions to keep discounts narrow, and second by falling asset values, the industry turned against gearing and against any instruments which caused dilution of the equity base. Many institutions either disliked the complications caused by warrant issuance, or in some cases were forbidden from holding warrants. The flood of investment trust warrants turned to a trickle, and then dried up abruptly. A few trusts tried attaching quasi-warrant convertible income shares, but the idea failed to catch on. Now there is little prospect of many new trusts issuing warrants, and it is difficult to see this merely as a cyclical shift in fashion. The terrible collapse of some split capital trusts, unwound by a combination of debt gearing, demanding income requirements, and cross-holdings, has tarnished the sector and made it nigh-impossible for trusts to complicate their structures with any form of exotic security – not least one which introduces gearing and the possibility of total loss. The number of investment trust warrants is slowly diminishing as existing warrants expire or as trusts restructure, and they are not generally being replaced. Whilst the long-dated nature of some trust warrants (for example, Aberdeen Asian Smaller warrants, which are scheduled to mature in November 2010) should ensure that warrants continue to exist in a minor way in the investment trust industry for some time to come, they have the standing of unwelcome guests who have lingered too long.

This is a pity – both for investors, and to a lesser degree, for the industry. For what it is worth, academic research indicates that trusts which attach 'free' warrants as part of an initial offering do create extra value. A 1997 paper by Gordon Gemmill and Dylan Thomas of the City University Business School in London, published in the European Financial Review, was quite definite about this point. Their conclusion was:

> "The results from examining 127 IPOs [initial public offerings] confirm that those issues which had warrants were more highly valued than those without. The increase in value did not occur at the time of issue, but only when the warrants were split-off and separately traded for the first time. It is therefore rational to include warrants when making new issues of shares, since these issues trade at a higher premium to net asset value."

The issue of warrants by other commercial companies has suffered a similar fate, as the UK has shifted towards the American model. In the late 1980s and early 1990s it was easy for British investors to scoff at the small US corporate warrants market, which was characterised by highly valued warrants of dubious quality and very thin liquidity issued by small, cash-hungry companies. The UK, meanwhile, could boast warrants from blue-chips such as Hanson, BTR, Pilkington, Lucas Industries, Anglian Water, and Eurotunnel. Now, with the sole exception of one remaining issue from Eurotunnel, these are all gone. And you've guessed it. They have been replaced by highly valued warrants of dubious quality and very thin liquidity issued by small, cash-hungry companies. It did not help that the performance of Hanson and BTR was poor as old-style industrial conglomerates lost their way, which left a sour taste as warrant holders again lost money. This diminished the attraction of warrants for other companies, who simply decided to leave warrants off the agenda. Except, that is, for those small cash-hungry companies who were able to use the issue of warrants as a form of reward for executives and shareholders, and as a deferred rights issue to boot. When company warrants are exercised and converted into ordinary shares at the end of their lives, the companies receive the exercise money, which can provide a welcome boost to cash reserves. Companies with carefully mapped expansion plans which require a continuing flow of capital investment can find it useful to have warrants.

Unfortunately for the warrants market in recent times, the most dynamic smaller company sector with entrepreneurial enterprises seeking cash for expansion was technology. A whole host of internet-related companies, mainly listed on the AIM, issued warrants as a path to extra cash, only to find the path disintegrating into crazy paving as the bubble burst, valuations collapsed, and companies lost their way. Nearly all of these warrants have expired worthless, or are set to do so, signifying a significant reduction in the quality of the UK company warrants market. Similarly, small AIM-listed mining companies have sunk plenty of dry wells for warrant investors.

Dealing spreads and liquidity have been other problems, exacerbated by the very small issues by 'penny share' companies. Fairly typical are the warrants of Southern African Resources – a 'shell' company with mining ambitions chaired by the former England cricketer Phil Edmonds. Its shares and warrants were listed on the AIM in London in May 2002. Each warrant entitled the holder to subscribe for one share at 1p between 30th April 2003 and 30th April 2007, and with the shares at 2.5p and the warrants at 1.5p the absence of any premium lent the warrants a superficially attractive air. Taking a closer look though, the dealing spread on the warrants of 1p-2p meant that investors needed a 67% rise in the warrants before breaking even – if they could buy any in the first place.

Lack of Rights for Warrant Holders

If that were not enough, it became increasingly apparent that warrants were often regarded by companies as something of an afterthought, or even a nuisance. Warrant holders' rights were sometimes treated in a cavalier way. Two examples from early 2002 sum up the problems which arose. First, where warrants are attached they are sometimes a minor part of a prospectus, and given little attention. Errors can creep in, such as in the prospectus for the AIM launch of the security company SectorGuard in March 2002. The terms of the warrants stated that "each warrant will entitle the holder to subscribe for five new ordinary shares at the subscription price of 3p per share", but more reading uncovered some inconsistency elsewhere in the document. After some prompting the company issued a correction to the Stock Exchange, restating the entitlement as just one share per warrant.

One of the important terms to check before buying traditional warrants has always been whether or not their 'time value' or premium is protected in the event of takeover. These provisions exist to ensure that warrant holders do not lose value if a company or trust is taken over at a price lower than that implied by the warrants. An example may help:

> • If a share price is 100p, and there are warrants carrying the right to subscribe at 100p in five years time, then the warrants might be trading at, say, 35p.

> • If an agreed bid is made for the shares at 120p, this is a 20% premium for shareholders, but warrant holders offered only the opportunity to exercise their warrants immediately would face a drop in the value of their investment from 35p to 20p (the takeover price less the exercise price).

This is clearly unfair and undesirable, and for this reason the vast majority of investment trust issues (but few company issues) have a standard protection formula which is built into the terms. This is in the format A=(B+C)-D where A is the reduction in the exercise price, B is the original exercise price, C is the warrant price, and D is the takeover price for the shares.

In the example given above:

> • The formula works out at A=(100p+35p)-120p, so A=15p, and the exercise price is reduced accordingly by 15p to 85p.

> • This means that the warrants have a value of 120p (the takeover price) less 85p (the revised exercise price), which is 35p – or equivalent to the pre-takeover price. Warrant holders do not gain under this scenario, but they do not lose out either, which is the point of the provisions.

So far, so good.

How, then, could the Aberdeen Emerging Economies investment trust announce in March 2002 that as part of the winding-up and unitisation of the trust they expected to pay approximately 8p in cash for each warrant when the market price was 15.75p? This announcement caused a considerable amount of anger and confusion. Unfortunately, the provisions in the documentation for these warrants were badly drafted and ultimately flawed. For a start, understanding the terms was very difficult. Lay investors were unlikely to comprehend the convoluted sentences and legalese, and even experienced warrant practitioners found it tricky to untangle the various clauses and sub-clauses.

In the terms of these warrants there were separate provisions which applied in the case of a unitisation or winding-up, as distinct from a takeover, and whilst these appeared on the surface to use the same formula, the small print was damning. The conditions were peculiar in that they assumed the warrants were exercised in full at the standard subscription price of 100p, even though this would clearly not have happened as the warrants were out-of-the-money (the share price was below the exercise price). This was both illogical and unrealistic, and the confusion was compounded by an assumption later in the calculation that the trust received the subscription money from the adjusted subscription price. There was an obvious inconsistency in that the exercise price was unequal on the two sides of the equation, penalising warrant holders. This was a flaw, and a flaw replicated for a number of other trusts.

Some investment trust warrant holders are likely to lose out materially when an investment trust with out-of-the-money warrants is wound-up or unitised, which is a ridiculous position. Short of suing the advisers to these trusts, however, who originally drafted and cleared the wording, there is little to be done. Ian Sayers, the technical director of the Association of Investment Trust Companies (AITC) summarised the problem neatly:

> "Warrant holders are not afforded the same rights and protection as shareholders receive under company law. Their rights are pretty much as set out in the warrant deed and, whilst the board must clearly ensure that the terms of the deed are complied with, they do not owe warrant holders the same general duties as they do to shareholders."

From the actions of the board of Aberdeen Emerging Economies, it would seem not. Warrant holders voted against the unitisation plans, blocking the proposals, whereupon the board moved to wind-up the trust anyway without a warrant holders' vote. The feeling that warrant investors were being treated as second-class citizens hardly served to enhance the standing of warrants in the investment community, and this extraordinary episode drove more investors away from the market.

Dead, or Only Resting?

So the quality of the market has been dropping, as has the quantity. By the middle of 2002 the number of warrants had declined to just 120, capitalised at £291m, from more than twice as many with an aggregate market capitalisation over a billion pounds some six years earlier.

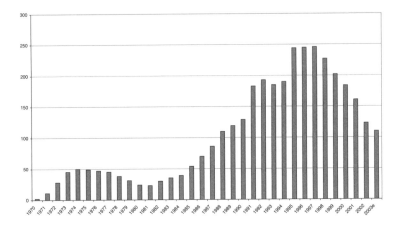

Fig 3.1 - Number of UK equity warrants listed on the London Stock Exchange, 1970-2003

This is not to say, however, that there are no good company or investment trust warrants available now. There are diamonds in the rough. Luminar is a fast-growing company which has used warrants to reward its employees; Scottish Oriental Smaller Companies trust warrants leapt by more than 75% during a tough 2001; and a number of good quality investment trust warrants are currently trading on zero or negligible premiums. The absence of general demand for warrants has left the way clear for enthusiasts to buy warrants on cheap ratings, and using some fairly simple technical analysis it is a straightforward matter to identify some excellent value. Whilst the market may not be growing any more, and may have encountered some silly technical problems, the underlying merits of the instrument still hold good. There are some good warrants, good value, and good profits to be had in the traditional market. The disappointment is that these features are not found in the great abundance promised a decade ago. The benefits which come from greater choice and variety should be served instead by the new market in covered warrants. It should take up the slack nicely.

One final point before moving on is that it should be interesting to see what the impact the new covered warrants market has on the supply and demand for traditional warrants. It could have an effect either way. The negative argument is that investors will shun the old market once the new one opens up hitherto unknown choice, liquidity, and information. Why step backwards to encounter wider dealing spreads and frustrating dealing limitations? The positive argument is that the new covered warrants market will serve to switch a whole new generation of investors on to the merits of warrants. Those investors will then hunt around for the best warrants to suit their needs, and may be pleasantly surprised to find some very long-dated investment trust warrants trading on negligible premiums. Should demand filter back to the traditional market, it could stimulate some fresh issuance from companies and investment trusts – especially if their directors and advisers are amongst those benefiting from the educational drive introduced by the new covered warrants market. Company and investment trust warrants could be kicked into touch or kicked into action. Time will tell.

4. History and Development (ii) In With the New

Anyone anticipating the arrival of covered warrants in London has needed a large reserve of patience. The desire to have a thriving covered warrants market in the UK for private investors is not new. For nearly a decade the London Stock Exchange has nurtured a fledgling plan, recognising the popularity of these instruments elsewhere; and potential issuers have regularly trudged into London, found the regulatory environment unhelpful, and gone away again with a shake of the head. It took years of fast-paced development in overseas markets to persuade British regulators that the time had come to let the public try the taste of this forbidden fruit. The London Stock Exchange has had a professional market in covered warrants for a number of years, and some over-the-counter (OTC) warrants have been traded in London by professional investors, but the market has essentially been closed for business as far as private investors were concerned. Interested individuals have been like greyhounds stuck in the starting trap while the rabbit completes several laps of the track.

Regulatory Development

Now the Financial Services Authority (FSA) has belatedly realised that London needs to compete and that it is unreasonable to prevent British retail investors from investing in covered warrants. The FSA has introduced new rules to facilitate the listing of covered warrants as part of its objective to "seek to maintain the competitiveness of the UK markets for listed securities." This does not explain why it has taken so long when covered warrant markets have flourished elsewhere for so many years. It had long seemed anomalous that investors could write options or take out spread bets with very high risks, yet not invest in an instrument in common usage across Europe. It says something about the global momentum of covered warrants that the FSA should feel able to introduce these to the UK market at a time of falling equity prices, pension shortfalls, split capital investment trust woes, mis-selling scandals, and numerous other reasons to protect the private investor. The impetus for the introduction of covered warrants was considerable. The FSA's rationale was twofold:

(i) UK investors had already shown an appetite for other products with some similar characteristics, such as options and spread betting; and

(ii) it recognised the pattern of development for covered warrants elsewhere in Europe.

Even so, there was rightly a concern over the risks, because of the possibility of total loss, and so the FSA tiptoed towards the new market with tentative little steps. It first issued a consultation paper, CP81, in January 2001, followed by CP114 in November 2001, and then the target for the launch date was pushed back as difficulties arose when framing the regulations. The market was due to start in April 2002, but it was probably just as well that it was delayed. Sharply falling stockmarkets provided a backdrop of gloom and low investor interest which would quickly have muted any initial fanfare. Suitable though they may be for all kinds of markets, the current public perception of warrants is that they are bull market instruments which are simply too risky and dangerous in tough conditions when share prices are falling.

In late June 2002 the FSA published its new rules governing the listing and conduct of business for securitised derivatives – a new class of investment which includes covered warrants. The rules have two principal elements – the listing rules and the conduct of business rules. The new rules officially came into force on 1st August 2002, although the launch date for covered warrants was pencilled in for the Autumn of 2002 to give the issuers time to set up all of their systems to comply with the new rules – and for the Inland Revenue to resolve some last-minute questions over stamp duty.

The Listing Rules

In drafting the listing rules the FSA's intention was to create a regime which achieved a balance between investor protection and facilitating access to listed markets whilst maintaining the integrity and competitiveness of the UK market for listed securities. If the rules were too protective and inflexible then there would be no chance of a new market getting off the ground; if the rules were too lax then the FSA would be pilloried for exposing investors to all manner of mis-selling and ill-understood dangers. This was not an easy balancing act, and it did seem on more than one occasion during the long consultative process that the regulators would fall off the tightrope, but they have made it to the other side.

The listing rules set out all of the conditions under which covered warrants can be issued and listed on a stock exchange. It is too detailed a document to be covered exhaustively here, but it runs at length through all of the procedures for listing and the information which must be provided in a public form. One such section deals with the types of underlying assets which are acceptable. The underlying instrument must be traded on a regulated, regularly operating, recognised open market, save where the underlying instrument is (i) a currency; (ii) an index; (iii) an interest rate; or (iv) a basket of any of the above. In other words, the scope is quite broad to encompass exchange-traded shares, plus currencies, indices, and interest rates. Other products may also be considered by the UK Listing Authority. There are no restrictions on the style of the warrants themselves, as long as there is full disclosure in the documentation.

One intriguing possibility is a warrant on a warrant. Because covered warrants will be listed securities, in theory they could act as the underlying asset for another warrant. The idea of a compound call could be very appealing for gung-ho investors seeking very high volatility. And, in theory, there is nothing to prevent a triple-call: a call warrant on a call warrant on a call warrant. Or a call warrant on a put warrant.

One other element of the rules worth mentioning is that a retail securitised derivative must not be a contingent liability investment. This needs explaining. A contingent liability investment is defined by the FSA as "an investment under the terms of which a holder may be liable to make further payments other than charges when the transaction falls to be completed." It is the case with many derivatives, such as futures contracts, that investors can be called on to make additional payments beyond their initial margin payment if the underlying asset moves adversely. That is emphatically not the case with covered warrants. You cannot lose more than you originally invest.

The Conduct of Business Rules

The conduct of business rules apply obligations to authorised firms selling securitised derivatives to private customers. Originally these proved a stumbling block in the regulatory process because the FSA proposed to apply its existing conduct of business regime for derivatives, which practitioners felt would have strangled the new market. The prescribed risk warning would have been alarming because it would have incorporated wording for contingent liabilities which would clearly not apply. Fortunately, the FSA listened to the responses to their proposals which argued that securitised derivatives were in many ways closer to shares in their characteristics than they were to derivative products, and they revised the terms of the rules to reflect the hybrid nature of the products. The revised rules lay down the requirements for suitable risk warnings.

Further sections of the rules deal with the training and competence regime for firms giving advice on securitised derivatives, and the permission regime for firms wishing to conduct business in this realm. There is also some interesting cost-benefit analysis which examines the cost of implementing these rules. For the purpose of these calculations the FSA estimated that in the initial phase of development there would be between 10 and 20 firms likely to act as issuers of securitised derivatives.

Issuers

Covered warrants in the UK can only be issued by financial institutions of the highest standing. The FSA has defined an absolute eligibility benchmark for all issuers that they believe will ensure the integrity of the market. Issuers must be banks or securities firms authorised for the purpose. Do not expect to recognise all the names though: these are not necessarily household names, at least not in Britain. Issuing firms which have been active and highly successful in other European markets have adapted their models and procedures to match the new UK regulations. They have 'ported' their systems, and to some degree their specialist staff, from other European markets to London. It is a pity that no British banks have the capability to participate.

The stuttering, uncertain gestation period for the UK warrants market was exemplified by one moment of minor farce when the technical procedures for trading were defined by the London Stock Exchange (LSE). Their Central Warrants Trading Service (CWTS) was to be limited by capacity constraints, and whilst other warrants could be traded effectively off-exchange through other systems, CWTS was intended to be the flagship service. The LSE decided to hand-pick five leading issuers for the privilege of initial trading on the CWTS, namely Citibank, Goldman Sachs, JPMorgan, Macquarie Bank, and SG. Macquaries then decided that the costs were too high and that it would not participate at the market launch, swiftly followed by Citibank, who doubted whether the start of trading would be sufficiently active to justify the significant technical start-up costs. This did not matter in the scheme of things, as the market was still evolving at that stage, but it does demonstrate that this has not been an easy birth.

At the time of writing it seems that four issuers will begin on the CWTS, namely Goldman Sachs, JP Morgan, SG and Unicredito/Trading Lab. There are six issuers overall who have expressed interest in launching warrants from the beginning of the market. The remaining pair, Commerzbank and Dresdner Kleinwort Wasserstein, will issue warrants with a listing on the LSE, but with trading taking place away from the order book, with non-automatic execution. The wisdom of splitting the market at the opening, at a time when it would be preferable for all market participants to be pulling in the same direction, is open to question, to say the least. Still, all will be able to issue warrants and seek customers for them.

For more information you should contact the companies or visit their web sites, but here are some quick pen pictures using information from the potential issuers to give you a flavour of who they are:

Commerzbank is one of Europe's leading banks with a strong position at the heart of the new Euroland. Its headquarters are in Frankfurt. It has the backing of a EU510bn balance sheet and is able to provide a full range of financial solutions to all types of clients. As one of Europe's leading warrant houses, the bank offers hundreds of warrants covering leading international shares, local shares, and stockmarket indices. The Commerzbank Group employs nearly 40,000 people and serves over 5m customers.

Dresdner Kleinwort Wasserstein (DrKW), the investment banking division of Dresdner Bank, a member of the Allianz Group, provides a wide range of investment bank products and services to European and international clients including corporates, institutions and governments. It provides a full array of advisory and capital markets products including mergers & acquisitions (M&A) and advisory services, equity and debt underwriting, sales and trading, derivatives and research.

Goldman Sachs has been present in the continental markets for over a decade. It currently participates in the three largest by volume - Germany, Switzerland and Italy - and occupies a top three position by number of transactions. Further afield, Goldman Sachs was the first issuer to be present in Japan and has been the market leader since its inception. The firm currently has a product range of more than 5,000 warrants, certificates and structured products based on a broad base of international and domestic equities, indices and sectors. Its award winning web site offers cutting edge valuation and analytical tools that help investors find the right product to suit their needs. Goldman Sachs will be present at the launch of the UK market as one of the four issuers who are listing their products on the LSE's continuously quoted CWTS segment.

JPMorgan is a leading global investment banking house with a reputation built over 150 years. It is one of the providers of choice for investors in Germany, Switzerland, Italy, and Hong Kong. It plans to follow the same approach in the UK and offer investors the opportunity to trade an extensive selection of securitised derivative products, in real-time, at competitive spreads, in a liquid, transparent and orderly market. JPMorgan was named 'Derivatives House of the Year 2002' by Risk Magazine, and received 19 awards from International Financing Review (IFR) in 2001, including 'Bank of the Year' and 'Derivatives House of the Year.'

Société Générale Group is a leading French bank, founded in 1864, with an estimated 13m clients throughout the world. The investment banking part of the business is known as SG. It is a leading player in global warrants, having first issued them in 1989, and it has more than 7000 warrants present on 15 stock exchanges. It was named the 'Equity Derivatives House of the Year 2001' by International Financing Review (IFR), AsiaRisk, and Risk Magazine, and has already received the same award from the latter for 2002. The bank says that it is committed to being a leading player in the UK covered warrants market, and will bring over ten years' experience of issuing warrants to support an outstanding warrant product range with tight bid-offer spreads and high liquidity.

Trading Lab is a trading name for The UniCredito Italiano Group, the largest banking group in Italy in terms of market capitalisation. Trading Lab Banca is the personal finance laboratory of the group specialising in producing derivative products for retail clients, and is the leader in the Italian covered warrants market.

If the market proves successful in the UK, then more issuers are likely to arrive to muscle in and grab some market share. Generally speaking, the more issuers there are, the better for investors, as competition on both prices and services can become fierce. Banks and institutions such as Citibank, Merrill Lynch, Macquarie Bank, ABN Amro, BNP Paribas, Credit Lyonnais, Credit Suisse First Boston, Deutsche Bank, HSBC, Lehman Brothers, Nomura, and UBS Warburg will surely be watching from the sidelines to see how trading volumes grow.

Method of Issue

Covered warrants will generally be issued in a simple way. The listing particulars will be published, the issuer will announce the issue, and then the warrants will start trading on the London Stock Exchange. There will be no requirement to place any of the warrants before trading begins. Investors wishing to buy will therefore do so in the secondary market. Interestingly, the rules do allow in principle for issuers to promote new warrants through initial public offerings (IPOs), using the listing particulars with an application form attached. This mechanism seems unlikely to be used in the early stages of the market, but issuers may give it a try later when they are competing for market share. Once the educational process has had time to work, and covered warrants are developed into more exotic forms to control risk, and perhaps even to provide some guarantees or some income, the IPO route could even be used to channel business through independent financial advisers, with some commission payments built in. The FSA would undoubtedly take a keen interest in any commissions which could be construed as 'incentive payments' for any form of covered warrant to be sold to the public, but its general view seems to be that an adequate level of investor protection can be maintained through the use of appropriate risk warnings coupled with high levels of disclosure.

Time and Trading

Warrants traded on the London Stock Exchange order book system will be open for trading between 8:15am and 4:30pm, the same hours as for shares (those traded through the RSP Gateway must be for at least this time, but trading can also take place outside these hours). Market-makers, or committed principals as they are known by the LSE, will be obliged to provide two-way prices throughout the trading day and for the lifetime of the covered warrant. These will probably, but not necessarily, be the issuers. Constant reference to the length of life of individual warrant issues should not detract from the point that you can buy and sell warrants at any time. There is no minimum requirement for warrants to be held for any particular length of time – and certainly not until expiry. If you wish to, you can buy a warrant and sell it again five minutes later. The ability of warrants to post large price gains over short periods means that there will probably be a certain amount of day trading in warrants, and a few professional investors who will devote themselves closely to the market.

Investors used to dealing in shares with execution-only brokers over the internet will have to sharpen their reactions to deal in covered warrants. Whereas a request for a quote for a share price will be held for thirty seconds for you to confirm the deal or back out if the price is not as good as you had hoped, quotes for covered warrants will be held for only fifteen seconds. The leverage provided by warrant prices, and their propensity to move further more quickly, means that the issuers would be exposing themselves to too much risk if quotes had a thirty-second hold requirement. As it is, there are still concerns about the scope for abuse, so this point is likely to remain under scrutiny.

5. Types & Terms of Covered Warrants

It takes time for a sophisticated palate to develop, and the issuers are in agreement that it is best to begin with what are usually called 'plain vanilla' warrants. These are warrants with straightforward terms, a simple right to buy or sell an individual stock or index. Once the market develops though and issuers become more bold with their offerings, all kinds of varieties are possible. This chapter covers a number of varieties of warrants which have been issued in other markets, some of which might eventually make an appearance in the UK. One fact which leaps from the page is that the term 'warrant' is very broad and that this highly flexible instrument can be tweaked, tuned, and transformed to match a wide range of demands.

Calls and Puts

Using covered warrants you can make money if the market goes up, and you can make money if the market goes down. Investors familiar with spread betting or with traded options will understand this approach which allows a judgement to be backed either way, but ordinary share investors may not. As a consequence, however, of the protracted decline in share prices at the start of the new millennium, investors have generally become more aware of the benefits of downside protection or speculation. The concept of short-selling has made its way into the newspapers, although occasionally in a disreputable context, and there has been a move towards 'two-way' investing even in the conservative world of collective investments where hedge funds with the ability to sell short have become increasingly popular. In a world where fewer and fewer investors are thinking of their investments as long-term choices which will rise steadily over the years with some fluctuations along the way, the availability of both calls and puts is a welcome development.

That said, most investors will probably buy call warrants, which give you the right to buy an underlying asset. It is often easier to identify specific factors which might push the price of an underlying asset higher, rather than those which might drag it down, and the great weight of analysis is still directed towards this end. The clear majority of newspaper columns, stockbrokers' reports, newsletter tips, and other advisory material provides many more buy than sell recommendations. Moreover, most private investors are by their nature optimistic. When the market falls many investors treat it more as an opportunity to find the bottom so that they can buy in again, rather than as a chance to make money from the decline. Profiting from misery and hoping for bad news is not an approach with which all investors feel comfortable. Furthermore, the market has always risen in the long run, so call warrants have the tide of history with them, other things being equal.

Think of a put warrant as a 'reverse' warrant. It entitles the holder to sell the underlying asset, which means the warrant gains in value when the asset falls. When you purchase the warrant you are effectively forward selling the asset, and when you sell the warrant you are buying the asset back again. If you sell at a high price and buy back at a lower price, you have made money, hence the inverse relationship between the asset price and the warrant price.

Example of a put warrant

Put warrant carries right to sell one share at 100p.

Share price 90p; warrant price 10p.

Share price falls to 70p (-22%); warrant price rises to 30p (+200%).

Using a real example, when the share price of the German airline Lufthansa fell with world equity markets in 2002, some series of put warrants performed very well. The SG 20/09/02 put warrants on Lufthansa which gave the right to sell 0.5 Lufthansa shares at EU15 gained in intrinsic value as the shares fell from EU18.5 in mid-March to EU11 four months later. A graph illustrates the inverse relationship between the shares and the put warrants very clearly:

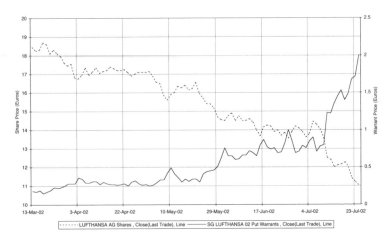

Fig 5.1 - Lufthansa shares and SG Lufthansa 02 put warrants, March-July 2002

40

Over the period covered by the graph the shares declined by 40% and the warrants moved up from EU0.18 to EU2.00 for an overall rise just in excess of 1000%.

For the reasons mentioned above, it may be that there is little aggressive buying of puts in individual shares, but this does not mean they will not be popular at certain times. They certainly have their role. Investors may be anticipating a general market fall, in which case an index put may be attractive, or puts can be used to hedge against a market decline. This tactic is explained in more detail in Chapter 11.

Very often, warrants will be issued as pairs. For issuers it is advantageous to offer both calls and puts for most warrant launches. To some degree the issues will cancel each other out, meaning that there is less need to hedge a large net position by buying or selling the underlying stock. One further benefit of the availability of both calls and puts for health of the warrants market overall is that this may smooth out some of the rises and dips in popularity and dealing volumes. Covered warrants can still prove attractive and make money in any market conditions, which means they have a place in even the most dismal bear markets as well as their more obvious application to amplify gains during bullish periods.

European and American

You may come across the terms 'European style' or 'American style' to describe the exercise terms of covered warrants. The distinction is straightforward. European style exercise means that the warrants may only be exercised on a specific date, or range of dates. American style means that the warrants can be exercised at any time up to their expiry date. In some markets there is an historic precedent which means that investors are more used to one style; or in some cases an issuer will always stick to one style, but neither seems to have any great advantage over the other. For issuers the European style is in some ways simpler because exercise occurs infrequently, or perhaps just once at the end of the warrants life. For investors the American style might be slightly preferable because it is more flexible for those who do wish to take up exercise rights, and because there is no distortion of the pricing curve. In practice, it probably doesn't matter too much. Few investors ever exercise covered warrants in any case, and the existence of a premium before final expiry usually makes it uneconomic to exercise American-style warrants early. If the simplicity of European warrants trims a few basis points from the premium, that is probably more valuable than an early exercise opportunity which is never taken up.

Warrants per Share

The traditional company warrants issued by Skyepharma on the London Stock Exchange, which expire in December 2002, have spent most of their life massively overvalued by most fair value measures. The reason is simple in that ten warrants are required to exercise into one share, and investors have failed to understand this – or even troubled to find it out in the first place. Nearly all of the traditional warrants listed on the London Stock Exchange are exercisable into their shares on a one-for-one basis. One warrant entitles the holder to subscribe for one share, and that is that. Investors began to assume this was the case, hence the confusion over Skyepharma.

This is not an assumption which should have been made, and certainly not one which should be made for covered warrants. The number of warrants required to exercise into one share, or its cash equivalent, could as easily be 0.5, 5, 10, or 100 as it could be one. This is frequently called the cover ratio, although it is also called the subscription ratio, the exercise ratio, the conversion ratio, the entitlement ratio, the parity ratio, the multiplier, the set, or just the plain 'ratio'. If 50 warrants are required to exercise into one share, the cover ratio is 50, or 50:1.

Cover ratios are rarely 1:1 for index warrants, nor for other securities which have a high absolute price. The purpose of 5:1 or 10:1 cover ratios is to reduce the covered warrant price down to an easily marketable and tradeable level. Historically this has been a necessity in markets such as Japan and Switzerland where the price of a single share can be beyond many investors.

When analysing any warrant, and when comparing different warrants, it is essential to check the cover ratio. If a valuation seems far too low or too high to be true, it probably is, and the answer may well lie with an incorrectly assumed cover ratio. A sensible approach when comparing warrants with different cover ratios is to ensure consistency by, for example, restating all prices on a 'per warrant' basis.

Stock Warrants

More warrants will be issued over single stocks than anything else. The majority of covered warrants are typically issued over the largest local companies, with a sprinkling of well-known global stocks to add an international dimension. In the UK the prime focus will be on constituents of the FTSE 100 Index, which are generally household names. The largest companies are BP, GlaxoSmithKline, HSBC Holdings, Vodafone Group,

Royal Bank of Scotland Group, Shell Transport & Trading Company, Astrazeneca, Lloyds TSB Group, Barclays, and Diageo. In that top ten, oils, pharmaceuticals and banks are well represented, but the full list provides exposure to a wide range of sectors. In the retail sector, for example, the index includes Dixons Group, Kingfisher, Tesco, Marks & Spencer Group, J Sainsbury, Boots Company, GUS, Next, William Morrison Supermarkets, and Safeway. The shelves are well stocked. Whether you want trolleys or technology, engineering or entertainment, drink or drugs, there are likely to be covered warrants available to meet your requirements.

Issues will not be restricted to the FTSE 100 and may filter down to some popular and interesting mid-cap constituents of the FTSE 350 Index. These shares are more difficult to hedge, so the issuer will need to be more certain of their popularity before making an issue, but it might happen. Possibilities include P&O, Easyjet, Railtrack, Celltech, Egg, London Stock Exchange, WH Smith, Logica, MyTravel Group, Stagecoach, Carphone Warehouse, JD Wetherspoon, Eurotunnel, Capital Radio, Selfridges, Tullow Oil, Xansa, Manchester United, PizzaExpress, Aberdeen Asset Management, and Autonomy Corporation to name a few.

Nor will there be just one warrant per company. Competing issuers may each issue warrants over the most popular stocks, such as Vodafone, with perhaps more than one series apiece. If Vodafone shares are trading at 100p then an issuer might issue a series of call and put warrants with exercise prices of 60p, 80p, 100p, 120p, and 140p to cater for investors with different gearing and premium requirements. By way of example, on the next page is a table showing 14 call warrants issued by Goldman Sachs on BMW in Germany. The range of warrants offers both in-the-money and out-of-the-money choices, a wide range of gearing levels, and some different maturities, allowing investors to back their views in a fairly precise way. It is common to have such a choice. In August 2002, each of the 106 stocks underlying warrants in Australia had an average of 13 warrants listed over them.

It is easy to see how the number of warrants in issue can quickly multiply, assuming there is a reasonable level of demand. This is especially true when markets have made a significant move in either direction, because certain series of warrants effectively become defunct as the price moves away from the issue level. In the example given, if Vodafone shares were to move substantially higher, to 140p, then further series of warrants might be issued with exercise prices of 160p and 180p to provide good gearing for the call warrants and more conservative in-the-money put warrants. This explains the apparent conundrum as to why the number of warrants in issue can rise sharply in very poor market conditions: it is because new warrants need to be issued with lower exercise prices.

Example of multiple series

BMW AG: Price: 39.25 EUR   06/08/2002

Strike	Expiry	Ratio	Bid	Offer
EU50	10.12.03	0.1	0.280	0.290
EU60	10.12.03	0.1	0.140	0.150
EU45	18.06.03	0.1	0.320	0.330
EU50	18.06.03	0.1	0.200	0.210
EU55	18.06.03	0.1	0.120	0.130
EU40	18.06.03	0.1	0.520	0.530
EU55	20.12.02	0.1	0.027	0.032
EU50	20.12.02	0.1	0.078	0.083
EU30	18.06.03	0.1	1.150	1.160
EU45	20.12.02	0.1	0.190	0.200
EU40	20.12.02	0.1	0.390	0.400
EU35	20.12.02	0.1	0.680	0.690
EU25	20.12.02	0.1	1.470	1.480
EU30	20.12.02	0.1	1.050	1.060

Some international company warrants will also be offered. Attention is likely to be focused on the largest and best known global companies, particularly those with brands which effortlessly span borders. Candidates might include Microsoft, Coca-Cola, Nokia, Total Fina Elf, Canon, Honda, Sony, Philips, Royal Dutch Petroleum, Boeing, Colgate-Palmolive, Dow Chemical, Exxon Mobil, Ford Motor, General Electric, Gillette, Hewlett Packard, Intel, IBM, McDonald's, Motorola, Pfizer, Philip Morris, Procter & Gamble, Texas Instruments, BMW, DaimlerChrysler, Deutsche Bank, Siemens, Telefonica, Bank of America, Cisco Systems, Dell Computer, Nestlé, Nintendo, and ST Microelectronics.

The argument long used in favour of investment trust warrants, that it is possible to form a sensible judgement about the course of a stable, conservative underlying security, and then back that judgement with a more exciting form of security, applies well here. For geared exposure to leading blue-chip companies these warrants may well be suitable for many investors. Certainly they will be an obvious choice for beginners. There is a huge amount of fundamental research available on the underlying companies, they are actively traded so the price moves frequently, and novice investors will have little difficulty in understanding the terms. There is nothing too complex about the majority of single-stock issues, and they represent a viable alternative to either direct investment or to competing derivatives.

Changes to the Terms

Companies rarely stand still, and in planning their corporate finances there are a number of changes which can occur in the share capital. Rights issues, open offers, capitalisation issues (share splits), return of capital, share buybacks and the like can affect the value of underlying shares markedly. Covered warrant terms should be automatically adjusted for such activity, so holders need generally not worry about these events. Whilst there have occasionally been disputes over adjustments made for covered warrants in overseas markets, the process is usually smooth and is subject to regulatory control as well. In the UK the issuer must notify a Regulatory Information Service of any adjustment or modification it makes to a securitised derivative as a result of any change in or to the underlying instrument, including details of the underlying event that necessitated the adjustment or modification. Most of the time the adjustments are simple common sense: there is no legitimate reason for warrant investors to be penalised (or indeed, to benefit) because the underlying company has altered its equity structure.

In the case of capitalisations, the calculation of the adjusted exercise price (AEP) is simple:

$$AEP = EP * \frac{\text{No. shares before capitalisation}}{\text{No. shares after capitalisation}}$$

A rights issue is more complex, but the basic formula is that AEP is equal to:

$$EP * \frac{\text{No. shares before rights} + (\text{No. new shares} * (\text{rights price/share price}))}{\text{No. shares before rights} + \text{No. new shares}}$$

The intention is certainly to ensure that covered warrant investors are not disadvantaged by equity adjustments, and where the procedure is simple this aim is met effectively and easily. One grey area where doubts remain is in relation to takeovers, a matter to which we return in Chapter 10.

Basket Warrants

Basket warrants are issued over groups of securities. Usually the basket focuses on a sector, which can be valuable in a market where a lot of information, from sub-indices to stockbrokers' research, is organised on a sectoral basis. Analysts will often form opinions about the value of their sector as a whole, enabling clients to switch between sectors at favourable times. This can be a profitable approach, since companies within a sector often move very much in tandem according to the prevailing trends. A natural disaster will hit the entire insurance sector. Lower interest rates will help the building sector. Strong retail sales figures help the high street stores. Regulatory changes affect utilities. These sector warrants could almost be considered as mini-tracker investment trusts.

Within a basket, each underlying share will have a weighting to allow the calculation of the value of the basket itself. Very often this is no more tricky than allowing for one share per company in the basket, but it is important to be able to value the basket correctly. Otherwise there is the possibility of serious mispricing, as occurred with the Bankers Trust 2080 basket warrant issued in Hong Kong in 1997. This warrant covered the stocks China Merchants, China Everbright and Pacific Concord, and rose from 1.52 cents to 8 cents in the first ten days of trading as speculators piled in without analysis or any awareness of its true value. The warrants' implied volatility hit 500% compared with the normal valuation range between 30% and 60%, and gearing was negative.

Basket warrants are useful for investors prepared to take a view on a sector but perhaps lacking the in-depth knowledge of individual stocks required to pick a single share which may provide the best performance. They also carry a lower risk than single-stock warrants because the risk is spread amongst a few stocks. Below is an example of a basket warrant which was listed by Macquarie Bank in Hong Kong, this one over a group of Chinese automotive shares. Brilliance China Automotive Holdings sells minivans in China, Denway Motors is Honda's partner in the country, Qingling Motors produces and sells Isuzu trucks and vehicles, whilst Jiangsu Express, Shenzhen Expressway and Zhejiang Expressway are toll road companies in China's wealthier provinces.

Example of basket warrant

Call Warrants on 'China Auto Express' Basket of Shares

Issue size: 300m warrants

Launch date: 25th February 2002

Expiry Date: 14th May 2003

Type: European-style call warrant

Underlying: Basket Unit contains 1 share each of Zhejiang Expressway Co Ltd (0576.HK), Jiangsu Express Co Ltd (0177.HK), Denway Motors Ltd (0203.HK), Brilliance China Automotive Holdings Ltd (1114.HK), Qingling Motors Company Ltd (1122.HK) and 0.95 shares of Shenzhen Expressway Co Ltd (0548.HK)

Entitlement/Warrants Per Share (Basket Unit): 10

Reference spot (1 basket unit): HK$10.293

Strike price: HK$9.778 (95% of Reference Spot, or 5% "in-the-money")

Issue price per warrant: HK$0.2859

Premium: 22.773%; Gearing: 3.601x; Implied volatility: 57%

Settlement: Cash settlement

A basket warrant allows geared exposure to a sector or other group of securities without the need for multiple trades with the cost involved. Baskets offer a number of useful advantages, but they are not especially popular overseas, perhaps because they add a layer of complication over the most straightforward single stock warrants or the other most popular group – index warrants.

Index Warrants

Frequently the most actively traded warrants on overseas markets are index warrants. In Italy in June 2002, 60% of all warrant trades were concentrated on just two underlyings – the MIB 30 Index and the Nasdaq 100 Index. Used as a proxy for the underlying market, primary market indices such as the FTSE 100 Index in the UK, the Dow Jones Industrial Average Index in the US, and the Nikkei 225 Index in Japan have a high profile and are closely followed by a large number of investors. Whilst not everyone will have an opinion on the likely direction of BP, Barclays Bank, or Tesco, most investors absorb a good deal of information about the overall market, and enough to form a judgement. Index warrants are a quick and easy way to convert your market predictions into investments. Clearly it is impractical for most investors to buy each component of an index, so derivatives are an obvious avenue for exposure. Investors can already take positions on the FTSE 100 Index by using traded options, financial futures, spread bets, or tracker funds, so warrants will be competing in a busy market. This should help to keep the premiums down. Covered warrants on indices tend to be comparatively short-dated and actively traded by investors seeking short-term gains.

Whilst the FTSE 100 Index remains by far the most widely quoted market indicator in the UK, it is likely that warrants will be issued over a number of different indices. The scope will be international, and should also allow for some additional subtlety in terms of the market sectors – in the UK at least. The table on the facing page lists some of the indices most likely to attract warrant issuance.

The attractions of index warrants are easy to understand. An investor without too much specialist knowledge, for example, but expecting a general recovery in the technology sector, could buy a call warrant on the FTSE techMARK 100 Index, providing a geared return based on a range of large technology companies. The risk of an individual stock going bust is diluted, and the position can be established for less money than a direct investment.

The question remains about how exactly you buy or sell a market index. How are the indices used as the underlying asset for warrants? The index level is treated in the same way as a share price, and because the number is usually high, the cover ratio of index warrants is often set to a multiple such as 10, 100, or 500. An example helps to explain:

Example

Index at 4000.

Call warrant exercisable at 3500 with no premium (for simplicity) is 50p; cover ratio is 10.

Index rises to 4250 (+6.25%)

Warrant is worth (4250-3500) = 750 divided by cover ratio of 10 = 75p (+50%).

At end of life, warrant value is settled for cash.

Table of Indices likely to attract warrant issuance

Index	Market	Companies
DJ Euro Stoxx 50	Europe	Blue-chips
FTSE Eurotop 100	Europe	Blue-chips
FTSE Eurotop 300	Europe	Large & medium
CAC 40	France	Blue-chips
Xetra Dax	Germany	Blue-chips
Hang Seng	HK	Blue-chips
MIB 30	Italy	Blue-chips
Nikkei 225	Japan	Blue-chips
Ibex 35	Spain	Blue-chips
Madrid General	Spain	Blue-chips
FTSE 100	UK	Blue-chips
FTSE 250	UK	Medium
FTSE 350	UK	Large & medium
FTSE All-Share	UK	Whole market
FTSE SmallCap	UK	Smaller
FTSE techMARK 100	UK	Large technology
FTSE techMARK All-Sh.	UK	All technology
Dow Jones Industrial	US	Blue-chips
Nasdaq 100	US	Nasdaq
Nasdaq Composite	US	Nasdaq
Russell 2000	US	Smaller
S&P 500	US	Broad market

The principle is that simple, although of course in practice the warrant will have a premium, and there will probably be several series to choose from with different strike prices, plus put warrants as well. Settlement is always for cash, since it is not possible to deliver an index. For overseas indices there may be a currency calculation to take into account as well, such that the warrant price must be converted into the local currency of the index before calculating its value. This needs to be checked in the terms before buying any overseas index warrant.

Sometimes the cover ratio is expressed in a different way for index warrants: there may be what is called an 'index multiplier' which is the amount paid per point of intrinsic value. Although the terminology is different, warrants with an index multiplier work in the same way as those with a cover ratio. That said, it is a good discipline in cases where the terms might be less obvious to read the terms carefully and to consider how the warrant will perform under different scenarios.

Bond Warrants

Analysts and the financial press often refer to the choice between equities and bonds, and on occasions investors may be impressed by the arguments that bonds represent a particularly good or bad bet. Many equity investors have never bought bonds, however, and have scant understanding of how the returns are calculated, which ones are best, and how they are bought and traded. One answer is to buy a call or a put warrant on a mainstream bond. We will have to see if any are issued in the UK, but if so then warrants may well prove to be a useful way of gaining access to a financial asset which is otherwise oddly remote from the reach of private investors.

Commodity Warrants

Warrants are available on brent crude oil on some European markets, but do not expect the warrants market to extend to pork bellies, cocoa, soya beans, lead, nickel, silver, and jet fuel. Covered warrants are not a direct substitute for the futures markets, and will not be directed that frequently towards commodities, which do not generally attract much trading demand from private investors. On occasions warrants may be made available on commodities in the news such as oil or gold.

Currency Warrants

Covered warrants can be issued on currency pairs to allow investors to take a position on individual exchange rates. A call warrant on the euro against the yen, for example, would rise in value if the euro strengthened, and a put warrant vice-versa. If currency is merely an inconvenience which bothers you when you go on holiday, this might not be a sector to interest you, but there are all kinds of reasons why currency warrants can prove enticing.

First of all, there is purchasing power parity. Anyone who has travelled will have experience of finding particular goods to be very cheap or expensive when compared to their home, and sometimes currency rates seem completely misaligned. Visitors to South Africa following the extreme political unrest in Zimbabwe which forced the rand down sharply, for example, found that almost all goods and services from hotels to meals, from safari trips to souvenirs, seemed dirt cheap. The currency had become misaligned because of political tension, and investors who thought this might ease could have purchased a call warrant on the rand to back their judgement. Likewise, the Asian crisis of the late 1990s opened up new tourist markets in countries like Thailand, partly because the associated currency depreciation had knocked the purchasing power out of line. The Economist famously constructed a 'Big Mac' index to compare purchasing power parity between countries, based on the price of a universally available standard good – the McDonald's Big Mac hamburger – and it is a useful measure of whether a currency rate properly reflects the relative price of goods within countries. If you have reason to believe that purchasing power parity may be temporarily out of line, then currency warrants could be a way to back your assessment.

Second, there may be personal financial reasons for dealing in currency warrants. Anyone considering the purchase of a new holiday home in warmer climes in Europe might agree to buy a plot from a developer, and then put the money aside for later stage payments on the property. Clearly there is a currency risk between sterling and the euro though, and an adverse movement (a fall in sterling) could make the property far more expensive than originally envisaged. Currency can be bought either spot or forward through a number of currency dealers who advertise in this market, but they are unregulated, which could cause a certain amount of unease. Banks quote very wide spreads between their buying and selling prices for currencies, so the solution could be to hedge using a covered currency warrant (a sterling put or a euro call) to 'lock in' the current rate. Comparatively little capital would be required for this, and it could provide peace of mind such that any adverse movement on the property front would cancelled out by a gain on the warrant, and vice-versa.

Exotics

Issuers will keep things simple in the UK to begin with, but it is only a matter of time before we see designer derivatives. Warrants are flexible instruments which do not have to conform to completely standardised terms like options: they can be issued over a wide range of instruments, with a wide range of exercise prices, and with a wide range of special conditions. When warrant terms are made more complex, these warrants are usually called 'exotics', and naturally they appeal to the more experienced practitioners in the market. It is wise to exercise caution when considering exotic warrant structures. The most important rule is as always to make sure you completely understand the product before you invest. Ignorance is not bliss, it is simply a fast-track to ill-informed decisions and losses.

Barrier Warrants

One development of plain vanilla calls and puts is to add a price barrier to the terms. This style of warrant can also be called a capped warrant. The usual idea is that in addition to the usual terms including an exercise price and maturity, a barrier level is also incorporated, which can be high or low. Once the barrier price is hit, the warrant expires immediately, either providing a capped return, or in the case of 'knock out' warrants, no return at all.

Call barrier warrants can be 'up and out' warrants which may expire early if the asset level equals or exceeds an upper barrier level. In this circumstance a maximum return is payable. They can also be 'down and out', which means the warrants expire early if the asset level equals or falls below a lower barrier level. This can mean that the warrants will immediately expire worthless, or if the exercise price is below the barrier level, that a minimum payout is made. Put warrants can use similarly structured barriers.

The rationale behind these warrants is difficult to comprehend at first, since one of the main attractions of warrants is that they offer unlimited upside potential. They also offer a fixed period of time for the asset to move in the right direction. Why cap your gains or, even worse, willingly agree to a barrier level which might suddenly truncate the exercise period and cause the warrant to expire worthless? The answer is that these warrants can be made available more cheaply, at lower premium levels, so in effect some flexibility and potential gain is traded for a lower initial price. As a consequence, barrier warrants usually move more for a given change in the underlying than plain vanilla equivalents.

If, for example, you are moderately bullish about a stock currently trading at 100p, and you think it will reach 120p, but not a price as high as 150p, then an 'up and out' call warrant with a barrier of 150p might offer good value. The existence of the barrier may diminish the premium you need to pay for the warrant, yet the barrier is set at a level which has no impact on your strategy, since you would take a profit on the warrant at a lower level if your target price of 120p is met.

There are also 'knock in' barrier warrants where the breach of a barrier level causes a change in the terms of the warrants. Barrier warrants are highly individual by nature, which is a good point at which to repeat the mantra that it is essential to check individual term sheets for precise details.

Corridor Warrants

Players of ten-pin bowling will have no trouble understanding the concept of corridor warrants. If the ball strays from the lane and into the gutter, your turn is over. The longer it stays in the lane the better your chance of a strike. Essentially, corridor warrants are designed to take advantage of times when investors believe an asset price will trade within a narrow band, remaining fairly static. They have in the past been called AIR corridor warrants – accrue income in range. The longer the asset stays within that band, or corridor, the more value is accrued and the more the warrant is worth. Usually a set payment will be made for each day the asset value stays within the specified band, up to a final maturity date. Effectively these are a development of barrier warrants – in this case there is both an upper and a lower barrier.

Example

SG Dow Jones Corridor Warrants; spot index level 10,200

First listed September 10th 2001 in Amsterdam

Tranche A: corridor 9500-11,500; issue price EU4.08; pay out EU0.05 per day in range; maturity 04/02/02

Tranche B: corridor 10,000-11,000; issue price EU2.77; pay out EU0.05 per day in range; maturity 04/02/02

These examples illustrate a number of points. Tranche B, with a narrower range, is offered at a lower price, but has a lower chance of accruing income from the tighter range. The maximum return for each warrant is EU5.00, for the 100 trading days multiplied by the daily income of EU0.05. These warrants are not ones to buy for the prospect of large returns. The break-even point for Tranche A is that the Dow Jones stays within the 9500-11,000 range for at least 82 days; the break-even point for Tranche B is that the Dow Jones stays within the 10,000-11,000 range for 56 days.

Trigger Warrants

Trigger warrants are not common, but they are possible. These warrants specify a particular event in their terms, such as the underlying asset reaching a specified level. If the trigger event occurs then a fixed payout is made; and if not the warrant expires worthless. These 'all-or-nothing' warrants have a lot in common with a straightforward wager. Warrant analysts will not generally encourage comparisons with horse racing, or with Russian roulette, but in this case they might not be entirely without validity.

6. Pricing and Trading

Writing about a market which has not yet started is tricky. Plenty of proposals have been published, but of course this section is based on preliminary information which may change, or have changed by the time you read this book. Be cautious. If you intend to rely on any of the details contained in this chapter, you should check them first to make sure they still apply.

If you are new to warrants, a short spell of dry or ghost trading, using theoretical rather than actual money, is not a bad idea before you dip your toe into the water. Use your investment process to select some warrants, and run a theoretical portfolio for a few days or weeks. This should help to iron out any stubborn creases in your understanding of how the process works, and by following the prices of your chosen warrants you can become used to the degree of price movement. You will also be more able to gauge your chances of success. This process is not perfect, because the emotions which can accompany the use of real money are absent, but it can still be a useful idea. Using your hard-earned money to invest or speculate with warrants is not a decision you should take lightly.

Warrant Information

First things first. Once you have found the warrant you would like to buy, you need to find it and to check it is the right one. Given the possibility that warrant issuance could extend to thousands if the market proves popular, a simple three or four-letter ticker symbol like those used for shares and equity warrants will not suffice. The LSE is proposing a standard format for short names for covered warrants, encapsulating key information in a concise and standardised way. There will be six elements to the data, in this order:

1. Underlying instrument identifier

2. Issuer identifier

3. Contract type (call or put)

4. Expiry style (American or European)

5. Sub-type (for exotic warrants)

6. Issue identifier for series of warrants

As an example, a Vodafone European-style call warrant issued by ABCD bank which was the second in a series with different exercise prices might have the code VOD_ABCD_CE_B. An American-style put, barrier, covered warrant on the FTSE 100 Index, issued by WXYZ bank for the first time, might be named F100_WXYZ_PAB_A. These might seem long-winded compared to ordinary equity codes, but of course this extra information is both important and necessary.

Covered warrants also require further data. Another five variables will also be disseminated with each warrant in the long name, namely:

1. Exercise price

2. Ratio (number of covered warrants to underlying)

3. Expiry date

4. Further info about expiry – which price will be used (close, last, VWAP)

5. Expiry settlement type (cash or stock)

The fact that all of this information will be readily and reliably available is a boon to potential investors. For traditional listed warrants this information has been much more difficult to obtain, usually requiring reference to the original listing documents. This hurdle has been cleared with ease, and these primary factors which determine the value of a warrant will be provided at the outset.

In other markets this information is also provided as a matter of course prior to the start of trading. On 24th June 2002, for example, the Helsinki Stock Exchange announced the terms of several warrants which were due to be listed on 26th and 27th June, all with a similar format:

Trading code:	3UUPMEW350
ISIN code:	FI0009607279
Warrant name in HETI system:	UPM3U19E35.00R.1SHB
Underlying:	UPM-Kymmene Oyj (UPM1V)
Issuer:	Svenska Handelsbanken AB
Warrant type:	European put warrant
Exercise price:	35.00 EUR
Last trading day:	19/9/2003
Date of expiration:	26/9/2003
Ratio:	0.1 (shares/warrant)
Round lot:	500
Number of warrants max:	100,000,000
Settlement:	Cash settlement
Additional information:	www.handelsbanken.se

One point worth noting from this information is that the last trading day is not the same as the expiry date. This does vary between markets – on Euronext, for example, warrants listed in Paris and Brussels may stop trading six days before the expiry date, whilst it is three days in Portugal, and in Amsterdam warrants are usually traded right up to the expiry date.

Pricing

Not all covered warrants in London will be priced in the same way, although to an end-user investor the difference may prove to be minimal. A limited number of warrants will use the Central Warrants Trading Service (CWTS) platform, or order book, which provides for fully-automated trading. This is a new segment on SETS, the exchange's electronic order book. This service provides continuous execution which means that two-way prices are continuously quoted, and a broker simply executes against the bid or offer as desired. You can check the price at any time and deal instantly.

Unfortunately the capacity on this system is limited for technical reasons, and as a matter of operating prudence. The LSE is fearful of running before it can walk. To some observers, it is starting at a crawl. This is rather disappointing, if understandable. For the London Stock Exchange to expand its coverage from around 4000 securities by adding large numbers of covered warrants at a stroke (the initial capacity on the CWTS will be only 100 warrants, but rising quickly to 1000 warrants) is a big step for an organisation which is resistant to rapid change. After all, it took the AIM, which has been quite successful, seven years to reach 700 companies. And above all, the systems must be robust and able to cope. Extra capacity can be added later once the systems are proven. The over-riding imperative must be to create and maintain confidence in the system's ability to cope with whatever price volatility and dealing volumes may be thrown at it. In any event, the considerable limitations of the CWTS do not place a cap on the number of covered warrants which can be listed. It seems likely that many covered warrants will be traded outside of the CWTS order book, using Retail Service Provision (RSP) facilities. Covered warrants can be listed, but have their prices displayed through other mechanisms, and this is the function of RSPs or the RSP Gateway system which is used by stockbrokers.

The retail stockbroking market in the UK is facilitated by an increasing number of Retail Service Providers (RSPs) who offer electronic pricing and execution services to private client stockbrokers. RSPs work by receiving real-time price updates from the LSE and from some or all issuers, and then offering trading to registered agency brokers at the keenest price. In July

2002 the LSE introduced its new RSP Gateway service which offered a centralised routing system for consolidating the various electronic links between stockbrokers and RSPs. This helps best execution, although it is too early to say whether it will be widely adopted.

This RSP system for covered warrants will not offer automatic execution, but will be a quote request system where an indicative quote may be displayed but the principal (or market-maker) is not obliged to deal until a quote is requested. In practice this should be fairly automatic, as long as the system works properly. There were concerns that for these warrants the prices would not be disseminated, effectively killing them off as a practical proposition for investors who would of course want to follow the price. In addressing this issue, the issuers explain that the price will be published for each deal, plus an end-of-day closing price, plus indicative pricing on information systems such as Reuters and Bloomberg. And there is no need to worry if you don't have a Reuters or Bloomberg screen. Their data is circulated, or re-circulated by third party data providers such as Onvista, who expect to provide this information directly to private investors on the web.

Some doubts remain over whether all stockbrokers will offer immediate access to warrants traded through RSPs as well as the CWTS, but any initial teething troubles are likely to be ironed out as business follows the demand. There is a two-way battle for business between those issuers who have decided to swallow some high costs and issue on the CWTS, and those who will issue warrants, probably in greater volume, outside of the order book system. Whilst no-one would really have wished the market to have started with a hotch-potch of different systems, this set-up will at least enable the market to get going and for the LSE to formulate a more coherent system later. Other overseas markets such as Euronext and the Bolsa de Madrid have updated and improved their systems once volumes grew. Waiting for a perfect system in London might have meant another decade without access to covered warrants at all.

The prices quoted for covered warrants will be firm in at least the normal market size (NMS) specified by the London Stock Exchange. The NMS is specified according to the following price bands:

Price	NMS
< 10p	100,000
≥ 10p < 50p	50,000
≥ 50p < £1	20,000
≥ £1 < £2	15,000
≥ £2	5,000

A rough rule of thumb is that deals of £10,000 or less will be waved through. From £10,000 upwards the principal may not necessarily be obliged to accept the deal, although in most cases it should be possible to trade in far greater size: the NMS is really just a starting point. Liquidity should not ordinarily be an issue in the covered warrants segment.

The 'tick size' has also been specified in advance. The tick is the smallest amount by which the price can move, and is again defined in bands:

Price	Tick Size
< 10p	0.25p
≥ 10p < £1	0.5p
≥ £1	1p

These tick sizes will apply for all covered warrants traded on the order book CWTS; for warrants traded on alternative services such as the RSP Gateway the tick size will be 0.25p for all warrants. The tick sizes apply to all currencies, so if the warrants are priced in euros then the minimum tick size would be 25 euro cents.

Market-making

These basic technical features all seem fine and logical; some other features of pricing may, however, prove more taxing for investors expecting covered warrants to function in the same way as corporate warrants.

The first puzzle is how the price is actually arrived at, because the forces of supply and demand take a back seat. Ordinarily, for equities and for traditional listed warrants, the price is purely a function of the demand from buyers and the supply from sellers. If there are more buyers than sellers then the price will rise to redress the balance, and vice versa. Either there is an order book where the best bids and offers are automatically displayed, or competing market-makers will make a price in each security.

For covered warrants it is different. The issuer will usually be the sole market-maker, or committed principal, who is obliged to make a two-way price in the warrant throughout the trading day. And supply and demand are, most of the time, only tangential factors in setting the price. Instead computers use algorithms to move the price automatically in relation to the changes in the underlying asset. There are too many warrants to price manually, and because covered warrants are a synthetic creation there is no need to balance supply and demand because the quantity in the market is more fluid.

In the case of an equity, if there are one million shares in issue, and there is buying demand for 100,000 shares, the market-makers will move the price up to attract sellers of 100,000 shares: they cannot release any extra shares to meet the demand. With covered warrants an issue will normally be for a large quantity of warrants which the issuer will hold and then sell to those who wish to buy them as the demand arises. The issuer will then make a price linked to the underlying asset, not related to how many warrants have been taken up by market demand. Fair enough, but alarm bells are ringing. What is to stop the issuer from fixing the price to the detriment of investors? What is to stop the issuer from widening the dealing spread to prevent sensible dealing during times of financial stress? And how are the prices really determined?

The single market-maker model, where only the issuer makes a price in its warrants, is a tried and tested approach in overseas warrants markets, and it works well without abuse. Competition is not absent: far from it. It is simply that the competition occurs across warrants rather than within each individual security. Competition is inter-warrant rather than intra-warrant. It is also reputational. On a popular security, warrants may be issued by several issuers, all competing for business. If one has a price which is less favourable than the others, it will very quickly become apparent in the market – good sources of electronic information make the process of comparison quick and efficient – and that issuer will lose out on trade.

Similarly, if an issuer were to behave badly and fail to provide a good service to investors, this would again become known in the market, and that issuer would find it extremely difficult to participate and issue warrants at all. The twin forces of inter-warrant competition and reputation work to ensure an orderly and fairly-priced market for investors.

Interestingly, the EUWAX market in Stuttgart takes this process one step further with a name and shame approach to market violations. The EUWAX system uses 'personal order guides' to execute deals rather than having an electronic order system with automatic order matching. Order executions, quoting obligations, and dealing spreads are all monitored, and phone calls are recorded. The exchange can fine participants for any breaches, but perhaps more effectively it publishes a monthly report detailing all violations.

As the exchange notes, none of the issuers or personal order guides wish to have the lowest ranking in this report since "it will have a direct impact on their acceptance by investors and market participants, and ultimately on their commercial success."

Price Influences

In deciding what the fair price is, the issuer will take a number of factors into account in the pricing model. Price determination is a sophisticated process which is largely undertaken using algebraic techniques and computer models. The five principal inputs are the asset price, volatility, time to expiry, dividend yields, and interest rates.

Factor influencing warrant price	Impact of rise in factor on warrant price	Impact of fall in factor on warrant price
Asset price	Rise (calls); fall (puts)	Fall (calls); rise (puts)
Volatility	Rise	Fall
Time to expiry	Rise	Fall
Dividend yields	Fall (calls); rise (puts)	Rise (calls); fall (puts)
Interest rates	Rise (calls); fall (puts)	Fall (calls); rise (puts)

The most important, but not the only, determinant will be the underlying asset price, which for call warrants will push the price of the warrants higher as the asset rises – they will move in the same direction, other things being equal. For put warrants the prices should move in opposite directions. This need not always be the case, however, because other things do not remain equal. It is possible for other factors to have an impact which overrides that of the asset price, although this is unusual. A call warrant could fall in value even if the asset price rises, if time has passed, interest rates have fallen, and volatility has dropped.

The volatility of the underlying asset is important. The higher the volatility, the greater the chance of profit on the warrants, so higher volatility means a higher warrant price.

Third, there is the time to expiry. The premium, or time value will fall as the final exercise data approaches, and as time passes so there is less opportunity for the asset price to move to produce a profitable outcome.

Thus, longer-dated warrants will generally achieve a higher price than short-dated ones.

Fourth there are dividend yields. The higher the yield, the lower the price of a call warrant, and the higher the price of a put warrant. Dividends are like slivers of capital value being sliced off and distributed.

Fifth, there are interest rates. It may not be immediately apparent what their impact is, but as interest rates rise, so will the price of call warrants. The reverse is true for put warrants. This is best understood by reference to the issuer's hedging strategy. For a call warrant, the issuer may have to cover the position by borrowing capital to buy the underlying asset. Clearly, the higher the interest rate, the higher the issuer's costs, which would be reflected in the premium charged for the warrant. For puts the reverse is true as the issuer may be able to hedge the position by selling the underlying asset for cash, receiving interest as a result.

Bid-only and Offer-only Warrants

Covered warrants will normally have a bid (selling) price and an offer (buying) price, but there may be occasions when warrants become either bid-only or offer-only. Warrants can become bid-only, or unavailable for buying, when a particular issue has become very popular and the entire tranche issued has sold out. In these circumstances, the issuer, still keen to transact the business, will commonly issue another tranche of warrants with the same or similar terms. Sometimes this will not be desirable, however, if the time remaining is short, or if the market price has moved substantially so that the exercise price is no longer appropriate for a new issue.

When a warrant becomes bid-only, the forces of supply and demand come into play and usually push the price of the warrant higher than it would otherwise be. For existing holders this is beneficial.

Of more concern is the position when a warrant becomes offer-only: in other words, you cannot sell them back to the issuer. The proposed London Stock Exchange rules, at the time of writing, indicate that principals are under no obligation to quote a bid price when a covered warrant has no intrinsic value. This is intended to protect issuers against the necessity to quote a 0.25p bid price even for a warrant which has no chance at all of achieving any value, but the broad drafting is a worry. Whilst the issuers would undoubtedly say that they would have no intention of avoiding their obligations to make both a bid and offer price, except in unusual circumstances, the fact remains that they could.

Exercising Warrants

Most covered warrant investors will never exercise a warrant. Whilst the value of all warrants is derived from their exercise terms, the majority of trades occur within warrants' lives, with investors trading in and out and taking their profits or losses before the final maturity date. Unless your aim is to buy the underlying investment, in the case of physically-settled warrants where the exercise price is paid in exchange for the asset, it will rarely be in your interests to complete the exercise notice and stump up the extra cash.

For American-style covered warrants which allow exercise at any time before their final maturity, it is unlikely that it will be in warrant holders' interests to take up the exercise opportunity early. The existence of a premium on the warrants which gradually diminishes throughout the warrants' life means that selling in the market is normally a better decision than taking up exercise rights. There may be some other factors at work, though, and there could be circumstances where early exercise would make sense. Take, for example, a stock-settled American style warrant which has been very successful and which has a small premium. An investor who wants the underlying stock, which is about to pay a dividend, and where a capital gains tax liability will ensue if the warrant is sold rather than exercised, may determine that some cost in the form of the lost premium is worth paying. In general, however, the only time it normally makes sense to exercise is at the final date, and even then an immediate market sale may be easier.

Cash Settlement

The large majority of UK covered warrants will be cash-settled rather than stock-settled. This means that the issuer will pay a cash amount for the intrinsic value of the warrants at the expiry date, or on exercise, if sooner. In other words, although the terms of call warrants are usually expressed as a right to buy, and put warrants as a right to sell, they are more accurately a right to receive a cash payment equivalent to the difference between the exercise price and the value of the underlying asset at expiry.

Example

Investor holds 5000 warrants with right to buy one share at 100p.

At final maturity date, shares close at 140p

Cash settlement = (share price – exercise price) * number of warrants

Cash settlement = 40p * 5000 = £2000

One small point which could get under the skin of warrant investors if it is not clearly understood is exactly which price is used to calculate the final value for a share at maturity. This needs to be checked in the warrant terms because it can vary and mean that the cash value on settlement differs from that anticipated. The potential for confusion arises because the closing price for shares traded on the LSE SETS system depends on what happens in the closing auction which takes place after 4.30pm. At this time an auction-matching algorithm is run, and if auction-matching takes place then a closing price based on this – labelled "UT" is used. If there are no transactions resulting from auction-matching, the Volume Weighted Average Price ("VWAP") of all automatic transactions from 4.20pm to 4.30pm is used. If there is no VWAP price (ie there was no trade in the last ten minutes of the day), then the last trade price prior to 4.20pm is used. What this all means is that a warrant trader with a keen interest in the closing price of a share cannot simply watch the screen at the official close at 4.30pm and jot down the price as the clock chimes on the half-hour. Closing prices can differ quite markedly from previous trades in certain circumstances.

An issue which might arise at some point is whether issuers might influence closing prices. In other markets such as Germany it has become apparent that the hedging activities of issuers have led to swings in the prices of underlying assets as the expiration date approaches. This should not pose too much of a problem as most warrant holders will sell out prior to the expiry. Bear in mind as well that most warrants will be issued over very large and liquid underlying assets, which means that the actions of one market participant should not have a great impact.

Stockbroking

It remains to be seen whether it will be a simple matter to deal in covered warrants through your existing stockbroker. Few advisory stockbrokers have the expertise to embrace the market fully in its development stages – although there are exceptions – and the large execution-only stockbrokers are providing mixed support as well. Some are keenly aware of the new market and eager to grab market share, complementing their dealing services with educational material and support for new investors. Others have simply turned away. This is a choice for individual firms, but for investors the key point is that there will be a sufficient number of enthusiastic brokers ready and willing to execute your business. Whilst not everyone is suitably enthused, the level of interest is already, before the market launch, at unprecedented levels.

Whether you choose to deal through an execution-only stockbroker or an advisory stockbroker is a matter of personal choice. You can always have accounts with both. The choice boils down to a trade-off between cost and service. Some investors, particularly those dealing over the internet, prefer an impersonal approach at the lowest possible price, and if you feel confident about your ability to deal effectively without help then this makes sense. Using a broker merely to execute and settle your trades is a commodity business, in which case all that remains is for you to buy that commodity as cheaply as possible. And there are some excellent deals available from highly reputable firms who will deal for as little as £10.

There are of course drawbacks with this approach. The main one is that you're on your own. Execution-only stockbrokers will not generally help with warrant selection – although some may produce guides and publications to assist you indirectly – nor will they discuss the merits of competing warrants, suggest when to take profits or losses, or provide you with anything above the basic service for which you are paying.

If you are a novice investor and would appreciate some hand-holding, or even for the broker simply to check that you are buying the series of warrants you intend, then an advisory broker can be worth the extra fees. If a canny broker well-versed in the ways of the market can prevent you from making one costly mistake, that might be enough to pay for the higher charges many times over.

Whichever style of stockbroker you use, you will have to sign a warrants risk warning notice before you can deal. This is a regulatory requirement.

7. Advantages and Disadvantages

There are advantages and disadvantages to covered warrants, and it is essential to be aware of both before investing. Only by considering both sides of the coin can you hope to make an informed judgement about whether these are the right instruments for your needs. A balanced view is essential – you will encounter reels of positive and negative spin in the press – so this section covers thirteen principal advantages and thirteen disadvantages.

Advantages

Gearing and leverage
Unlimited gains, limited losses
Ease of accessibility and transparency
Good liquidity
Low transaction costs
Designed as a retail product
Opportunities in bull and bear markets
Range better than ever before
Aid to diversification
Ability to invest in assets otherwise unavailable
Rational price movement
Stock exchange listing
Provision of information and education

Disadvantages

Complexity
Adverse price movements
Premium
Limited life
Time value decay
Absence of price anomalies
No income
Scope still limited
No benefit to, or direct link with, companies
No shareholders' rights
Need to have internet access
Capital gains tax
Credit risk

It is up to you to consider the arguments for and against investment and to decide for yourself whether covered warrants are a suitable place for your money. Warrants attract strong opinions for and against, often depending upon the personal experience of the person voicing the opinion. Most warrant experts will tell you that warrants are a superb vehicle for speculative investment, but that is little more than preaching by the converted. Read on and decide for yourself.

Advantages of Covered Warrants

1. Gearing and Leverage

More for less. It's an attractive proposition, and this is what gearing is all about. Gearing is the primary attraction of warrants, and it is this property which can magnify profits to a size unmatched and undreamt of by many other investments. Warrants are pure capital securities, and the capital gains they can achieve when things go well are heady to say the least. Even speculative forms of direct equity investment such as penny shares and technology stocks are unable to keep pace with some of the gains which regularly occur on warrant markets. Using warrants it is possible to make a small fortune, and occasionally a large one.

Buying covered warrants rather than the underlying assets directly means that you can gain access for a lower entry cost. Instead of buying a share for 100p you may be able to buy a warrant with a right to buy the share for a fraction of the price. For example:

• If some shares are 100p and a covered warrant carries the right to buy the shares at 80p, then the warrants might trade at 20p (assuming a zero premium for simplicity).

• A 20% rise in the shares from 100p to 120p means that the warrants must be worth at least 40p – a 100% increase.

This is the gearing effect (or, more properly, as explained in Chapter 9, the leverage effect). Essentially this reflects the lower price of the warrants, which means that absolute changes are proportionately greater.

In general, the gearing property of warrants means that price changes in covered warrants will exaggerate movements in the underlying assets. A graphical illustration is useful. This example uses the shares of the German sporting goods company Adidas-Salomon and a DZ Bank 17/09/02 call warrant carrying the right to buy 0.1 shares at EU90 per share.

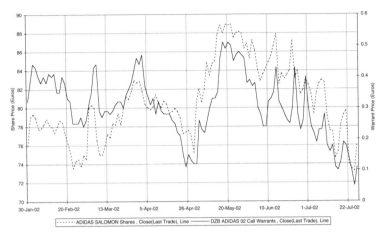

Fig 7.1 - Adidas-Salomon shares and warrants, January-July 2002

In this case the share price and warrant price seem to move very much in tandem, so where is the gearing benefit? The answer lies in the lower price of the warrants, which is masked by the double-axes of the graph. Looking closely at the price rally at the start of May 2002, for example, the shares rose from EU75.2 to EU88 and at the same time the warrants moved up from EU0.12 to EU0.51. Shareholders gained 17% over the fortnight, but the warrants rose by no less than 325%, magnifying this rise very significantly.

It takes some time to tire of positive examples, and a different form of chart illustrates the gearing more dramatically in any case. This example is another German stock, Thiel Logistik, which is a logistics company describing itself as "a comprehensive solution provider with logistics competence." In mid-July 2002 the company announced a decline in earnings for 2002 as expected, but also said that it would not need to lower its annual forecast any further in the current fiscal year, which pleased the market. This led to a partial recovery in the shares which had suffered a severe loss of confidence after two large shareholders sold substantial stakes the previous month.

Figure 7.2 plots the shares of Thiel Logistik and a series of Deutsche Bank warrants which rose by 354% over the month of July 2002. In this case the shares and warrants have both been rebased at 100 at the start of the period.

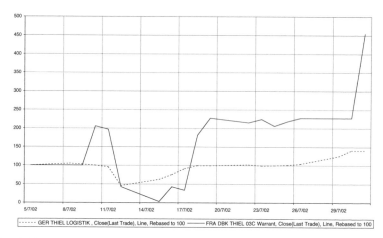

Fig 7.2 - Thiel Logistik shares and warrants, July 2002

The gearing benefit is obvious from this graph. In terms of making an investment, there are different ways of looking at gearing. The aggressive approach is to view the gearing benefit as a way to achieve a large equity exposure from a relatively small investment. Returning to the theoretical example of shares at 100p each, an investment of £5000 could have purchased 5000 shares, but that same investment could have purchased 25,000 warrants at 20p each. As each warrant confers the right to buy one share, this gives the warrant holder rights over 25,000 shares, worth £25,000. So in effect £25,000 of exposure is gained for an outlay of just £5000, and the greater exposure carries with it the possibility of a commensurately larger gain. This is sometimes called 'gearing up.'

You can also gear down. Using gearing defensively you can achieve an intended exposure for less money and less overall risk. An alternative to buying £5000 worth of shares would be to obtain the same exposure and the same profit potential through a purchase of 5000 warrants at 20p each. The total outlay is only £1000. This means that the balance of £4000 can be kept safe or invested elsewhere, and the maximum amount of money which can be lost is reduced from £5000 to £1000.

So, do investors generally gear up, or do they gear down? It depends upon individual mentality and goals, but on balance more investors probably gear up and go for aggressive growth with a small portion of their overall portfolio allocated for this purpose. Using gearing in this way can be highly useful for investors with a limited amount of risk capital but who are prepared to accept a high level of risk. And let's not be too prim. It can be tremendously exciting to invest in warrants, particularly for investors who enjoy playing the stockmarket as a gripping and absorbing hobby. It can be great fun to make your selections and watch them run. Is a 1% or 2% rise in a blue-chip stock really enough to set your pulse racing when you call up some pages on teletext, log on to the internet, or read your newspaper the following morning? Probably not. A 10%, 50%, or 100% rise in a holding of covered warrants, however, can be highly exhilarating, and the gearing element of warrants means they are far more likely to achieve stellar gains than the underlying assets themselves. The excitement factor can be high when investing in warrants, and for some investors this is what makes them so inviting.

Gearing tends to be much higher on average for covered warrants than in the traditional company and investment trust warrant market. In July 2002 the average gearing in the traditional London market stood at three times, whereas a study of 180 over-the-counter covered warrants at the same time, by the Covered Warrants Alert newsletter, found average gearing of 15 times. This might be why the top corporate warrant over the month posted a rise of 44%, whereas some Exane Peugeot 46.4 8/02 covered put warrants accelerated by 245%. High levels of gearing are available from covered warrants, which means potentially high excitement and high returns.

2. Unlimited Gains, Limited Losses

If you invest in warrants you may lose your shirt, but if things go well you can afford an entire new wardrobe. The combination of limited losses with unlimited gains for call warrants constructs a powerful argument. It is an attractive asymmetry.

If you invest £1000 in warrants then no matter how badly your investment turns out, you cannot lose more than £1000. Your loss is limited to the money you put in. It is a first-rate feature of warrants that your maximum loss is known in advance, unlike futures and, crucially, spread-betting. Sensational stories arise from time to time of speculators who have got in over their heads with spread-betting firms, and who have lost huge sums of money because markets went awry in a way they had not foreseen.

The Financial Mail on Sunday published an article in July 2002 about a spread-better who lost a small fortune when a series of bets placed earlier in the year on the medical technology company Biocompatibles International went wrong. In March 2002 the company announced that human trials of a key drug in the US had flopped and were likely to be abandoned. The shares tumbled from 147p to 74p, which was when the investor closed his bets at a total loss of £241,050. The article reported that the spread-betting firm was suing the man for the balance of the money which was not in his account. Spread betting, where investors bet that shares will rise or fall, effectively opens a position which means you make more profits as the share price moves in the right direction, or more losses as it moves the wrong way. Technically, the potential loss is limited to the point where the share price is zero, such that a £100 per point 'up' bet at 150p carries a maximum loss of (£100 x £150) £15,000, but this is likely to be a far larger sum than would be considered acceptable by the investor making the bet. The trouble is that unexpected events do happen, and they can result in massive losses which investors cannot afford.

Warrants confer a right upon the holder, but not an obligation. If the warrant is not worth anything at the end of its life, the right lapses and that is the end of the matter. No further action is required, no further payments, and no further loss.

Almost as important as the fact that the loss is limited when investing in covered warrants is the fact that the maximum loss is known in advance. It cannot creep up and surprise you. With covered warrants, you should never invest more than you can afford to lose. If it then goes wrong, you can afford it and pick yourself up without permanent injury. This should mean that you can invest with confidence without the terrible pangs of fear which can arise when your potential losses have no effective cap. It also means that covered warrants can represent a favourable alternative to shares in a circumstance where an investor believes an event will occur, but that the price will move adversely if it does not.

Consider a company which has been embroiled in a major court case which is reaching its final conclusion. The investor believes the company will win the case together with substantial damages which could provide a major boost to the share price, and wishes to back his judgement with exposure to £10,000 of shares. The investor is concerned, however, that if his judgement is wrong, the share price could fall sharply. The answer is to buy a highly geared covered warrant which means the exposure and equivalent profits can be gained at a far lower cost, and the loss limited accordingly. The same exposure might be gained through a purchase of covered warrants geared five times, which means the maximum loss is limited to £2000 no matter how badly affected the shares are in the event of the case being lost.

To see how this works, look at the example figures on the opposite page:

Share purchase

Share price 100p. Investor buys 10,000 shares, value £10,000.

Scenario A: company wins case, shares rise to 140p. Value of shares £14,000, profit £4000.

Scenario B: company loses case, shares fall to 60p. Value of shares £6000, loss £4000.

Covered warrant purchase

Share price 100p. Investor buys 10,000 warrants exercisable at 100p, price 20p, value £2,000.

Scenario A: company wins case, shares rise to 140p. Warrants rise to 60p, value of warrants £6,000, profit £4000.

Scenario B: company loses case, shares fall to 60p. Warrants fall to zero, loss £2000.

And yet with ordinary covered call warrants there is no cap on the potential gains. If you invest £1000 and your investment turns out spectacularly well, your profit might be £10,000, £25,000 or £100,000. It is an unequal equation between profits and losses, and it is in your favour. For put warrants there is a limit (albeit a high one) to the potential profit because the underlying asset price cannot generally fall below zero.

3. Ease of Accessibility and Transparency

To deal in covered warrants you simply need to ask your stockbroker, if you have one, or to open an account, which is generally a very simple procedure. It is not difficult to get started, especially if you are already used to trading in shares. Warrants essentially work in the same way, with largely the same method of dealing. Settlement is also the same as for shares using electronic settlement in CREST, with a T+3 (three working days) payment cycle for order book warrants. Trades away from the order book may have non-standard settlement cycles. All settlement will be dematerialised, which means there are no certificates.

Covered warrants are easily accessible, and the market has the considerable benefit of transparency. You can see what is going on, which means you can also see whether you are getting a fair deal. This is not always true in other markets. If you are taking out a spread bet, for example, how do you really know that you are dealing at the best price the market has to offer? There is no central trading platform, and without the time-consuming task of checking individual prices with each firm, the default is to rely on getting a fair price from your favourite firm, or simply the one with whom you happen to have an account. The market is opaque. In contrast, the centralised listing and trading arrangements for covered warrants mean that all prices are very easily accessible to enable a full comparison and choice. The market is fully transparent, right down to the reporting requirements which mean that trades must be reported within three minutes.

4. Good Liquidity

It has been a considerable frustration in the UK listed equity warrants market that it has been so difficult to invest decent sums. The average market capitalisation for each warrant of £2.6m restricts the number available in the market, and can make it tricky to invest as little as £1000 to £2000 in some issues. There is little point in learning about the market in detail, carefully analysing the warrants on offer, and making selections, only to find that the whole exercise becomes academic because you cannot actually put your cash in. This should not be a problem in the covered warrants market because the issue sizes are larger and because the pricing system is established with the issuer in a facilitative role. Larger investors should find a much warmer welcome from the new market.

5. Low Transaction Costs

The costs of dealing in covered warrants are not high. If the costs are broken down from start to finish, covered warrants score well on all counts, with a bulls-eye along the way. First of all there is the set-up cost before you deal, which is negligible. In many cases you will be able to use your normal stockbroker, or you can obtain the name of a new one easily enough, and there will be no cost to opening an account. Second, there is the stockbroker's commission on all deals. Charges should be exactly the same as for shares, which means that using an execution-only stockbroker you will be able to deal in warrants for as little as £10. Stockbroking is a highly competitive market.

The real kicker comes next. If you buy shares you have to pay a chafing 0.5% stamp duty charge, which vociferous lobbying has so far failed to have removed. This tax militates against successful short-term trading and is a considerable source of irritation to frequent traders and larger, more conservative investors alike. The good news is that most covered warrants will be free of stamp duty. For cash-settled warrants there will be no stamp duty to pay; stock-settled warrants will incur the usual 0.5% charge, plus a further 0.5% of the exercise price at expiry. Cash-settled warrants were the norm across Europe in any case, but this additional factor means that nearly all covered warrants in the UK are likely to be cash-settled – with good reason. Is this a big deal? Consider an active investor who over the course of a week decides to trade in and out of a warrant three times, investing £3000 on each occasion. The immediate saving is £45, which is not a fortune, but these charges do add up for frequent traders and mean that a larger profit is required on the investment to make it all worthwhile. There is also something satisfying about beating the taxman, which does not happen very often.

Pleasing though the absence of stamp duty is, it pales into insignificance alongside the dealing spread, which is a far larger component of the overall cost of dealing. And there is every sign that dealing spreads will be tight in the new market. For covered warrants, maximum spread rules will be applied to warrants traded on the order book, either the greater of 10% on the bid price or 1p, but in practice dealing spreads are likely to be far narrower.

6. Designed as a Retail Product

Covered warrants have been specifically designed for private, or in the industry parlance, 'retail' investors in the UK. Their introduction has taken place only after extensive regulatory scrutiny which provides the right levels of protection. The trading platform has been designed to be easy to use and to understand. Supporting literature has been written for the layman. Private investors are welcome and are in no way going to be treated as secondary to large institutional investors. It can be galling for private investors to play the role of the little guy powerless to stop large institutional holders from wielding their block votes to direct proceedings in their interests, as sometimes happens with ordinary shares. This should not happen with covered warrants, where trading is usually dominated by private clients.

The Financial Services Authority (FSA) has been anxious to mitigate the risks of investing in covered warrants as much as possible for private investors, which means strict regulations on the information to be disclosed in the listing particulars of each warrant. They must have a risk warning on the front page, and full descriptions thereafter of how an investor's return is calculated, the exercise rights and procedures, the nature of the underlying instrument on which the warrant is linked, where further information on the performance of the underlying can be found, and a description of events which may affect the underlying instrument. The idea is to ensure that a full disclosure is made to investors.

One subtlety relating to the listing particulars illustrates how seriously the law is protecting private investors to a greater degree than institutional investors. The listing particulars for covered warrants must include the following statement by the directors of the issuing bank that they accept responsibility for the information included:

> "The directors of [the issuer], whose names appear on page [page no.], accept responsibility for the information contained in this document. To the best of the knowledge and belief of the directors (who have taken all reasonable care to ensure that such is the case) the information contained in this document is in accordance with the facts and does not omit anything likely to affect the import of such information."

The names, addresses, and functions of these directors will be included in the document. This is a legal requirement which the FSA was not able to waive for securitised derivatives for sale to retail investors in spite of pressure from the issuers. For warrants issued to sophisticated investors the law is modified to allow this statement to be made by the corporate body of the issuer, which is clearly much less onerous. Given that the directors have personal responsibility for the particulars, investors can feel reassured that they will have been checked, re-checked, and then checked again.

A further regulatory requirement for automatic exercise of warrants in certain circumstances is another tremendous example of the thought and effort which has gone into making this market suitable for private investors. The finite life of covered warrants means that the final expiry is an important date – and a potentially costly one for neglectful investors. Consider this scenario. An investor holds a warrant with a right to buy a share at 100p, and the shares are trading at 165p. The warrant has a value of 65p as a result, but the investor misses the final exercise date and fails to exercise his rights to claim the cash equivalent of this value. Because the warrant expires, it becomes worthless, and the investor loses his entire investment – not through market performance, but through neglect. And this does happen. People forget, they go on holiday, they move house (or change e-mail address) and lose their mail, they fail to understand that action is required, or they never really understood what the warrant was all about in the first place. In the traditional company and investment trust warrants market, history is littered with examples of investors who have lost money by exercising their subscription rights at the wrong time, or not at all. Sometimes there is a safety net in the form of a trustee, but not always. Investors in Jupiter Global Green Investment Trust participating convertible shares (a form of quasi-warrant), for example, will be left with nothing if they have failed to exercise their subscription rights in time for the final exercise date in 2009.

The FSA regulations for the new covered warrants market recognise this potential problem and deal with it very satisfactorily. In the case of retail securitised derivatives, where the holder has a right of exercise the terms and conditions must provide that:

(a) for cash settled securitised derivatives that are in the money at the exercise time on the expiration date, the exercise of the securitised derivative is automatic.

(b) for physically settled securitised derivatives that are in the money at the exercise time on the expiration date, in the event that the holder fails to deliver an exercise notice by the time stipulated in the terms and conditions, the issuer will, irrespective of such failure to exercise, pay to the holder an amount in cash in lieu of the holder's failure to deliver such exercise notice, the amount and method of calculation of this amount to be determined by the issuer (the "assessed value payment amount").

Neglectful or inexperienced investors are caught by this safety-net to ensure that accidental loss of value does not occur. In regulatory-speak, from the FSA's proposed rules, "an effective method of protecting retail investors is to ensure that they are not penalised for any lack of experience in relation to the administration and procedural detail connected with the settlement of these products."

So private investors should be well protected, and well served in other ways too. Issuers will be battling for market share, which means they will want to create the kind of warrants investors want to buy. Shares and other assets which are popular with private investors are likely to be well represented in the warrants market. If a particular company is in the news, and there are no attractive warrants, you can expect some to be issued – and post haste. Issuers can move quickly and inexpensively. A new issue of warrants can be effected in 48 hours, and the initial admission fee is around £500 per warrant (although there are order and transaction charges thereafter, and FSA fees as well). We can also expect to see some innovative marketing in the structures. Basket warrants offering exposure to groups of shares, often in a particular sector, can be issued, which means that issuers can exercise their creativity. You might see a Windows basket of software companies when

Microsoft launches the next version of its PC operating system; a World Cup warrant for Germany 2006; a Harry Potter publishing basket when JK Rowling's next tome hits the bookshops.

This is a realm in which private investors really matter. Clients will be wooed by the issuers and protected by the regulators, and for many smaller clients it will make a refreshing change to be in pole position.

7. Opportunities in Bull and Bear Markets

This point has been explained elsewhere and should not require further elaboration. Using put warrants as well as call warrants means that certain warrants can prosper in bear markets as well as bull markets. Detractors who have always decried warrants as 'raging bull market instruments only' will have to think again. Covered warrants are more versatile.

Sceptics may argue that the availability of put warrants is of little value if no-one uses them. This may be a fair point, but experience in overseas markets is the same as for spread-betting in the UK. During extended downturns investors will begin to take short positions: the put to call ratio (the number of puts traded divided by the number of calls traded) in the Australian options market, for example, rose from 0.7 at the end of 2001 to 1.4 at the end of July 2002. Evidence suggests that investors do welcome the availability of put instruments, which are new to the warrants market in the UK.

8. Range Better Than Ever Before

The choice of covered warrants will be like nothing London has ever seen before. The warrants market in the UK has an opportunity to leap off its sick bed and return to rude health in one bound. For fans of the sector who have found the limited number of warrants a frustration, the idea of hundreds, or even thousands, of new warrants suddenly becoming available is a tremendous prospect.

9. Aid to Diversification

For smaller investors, the lower price of covered warrants can be used to help portfolios become more diversified. An investor with £5000 to invest in shares, for example, may decide that £1000 is the minimum efficient investment in each. The resulting portfolio of five shares will necessarily be concentrated and vulnerable to poor performance if the selections prove to be unfavourable. Using covered warrants, the same exposure to those five shares could perhaps be achieved by an investment of £2000 in total, or £400 per warrant. This allows the balance of £3000 to be used for further purchases which may broaden the sector or geographical base of the portfolio, lessening the dependence on individual stock performance and reducing overall volatility.

10. Ability to Invest in Assets Otherwise Unavailable

Warrants can also improve your investment reach. Using covered warrants listed on the London Stock Exchange investors should have the ability to play all kinds of markets and views, some of which were previously too difficult or expensive to consider. This is particularly true for warrants which may be issued on currencies, commodities, baskets of shares, and overseas instruments. Major international shares, for example, receive quite a lot of coverage in the British press, and are featured at length in analysts reports and on any advisory services with international scope. Yet it remains awkward to buy direct holdings in some of these companies, which will be brought easily within bounds by fully listed covered warrants.

11. Rational Price Movement

All stockmarket investors will know that the forces of supply and demand can be capricious. Prices do not always move when you want them to, and valuations do not always correct from irrational levels. The equity warrants market in the UK has produced numerous examples of warrant prices which have defied logic by shooting higher when least expected, suddenly collapsing, or even moving in the opposite direction to the underlying share price, which call warrants are not supposed to do. This is all very well if you are a canny market participant, but the majority of less involved investors prefer pricing to be a cool, rational process which can be subjected to sensible forms of analysis. The pricing system for covered warrants, where prices are based more on fair value calculations than supply and demand, means in general that logic applies. In turn this means that correct decisions are more reliably rewarded.

12. Stock Exchange Listing

Covered warrants will be listed on the London Stock Exchange and traded according to its rules. This unmatched legitimacy is a comforting background for investors risking capital by investing in geared products. It is a huge advantage over competing instruments such as spread-betting. For novice investors the choice between investing in a covered warrant listed on the London Stock Exchange, through their usual stockbroker, or opening a spread-betting account looks one-sided. Without wishing to disparage the spread-betting firms in any way, investors can feel confident that the LSE will maintain orderly markets with properly maintained bid and offer prices and spreads during good times and bad. The exchange claims to be the most international exchange by trading in the world, with Europe's largest pool of liquidity. At the end of 2001 the market capitalisation of UK and international companies on its markets was £4.1 trillion.

There is a trend in some overseas markets such as Germany for investors to begin trading directly with the issuers without the need for a 'middle-man' exchange. This can be quicker, with better functionality, and allows for longer trading hours, including evenings. This is not currently permitted in the UK, and seems unlikely to happen for some time, if at all. For regulators concerned about investor safeguards, the cushion provided by the LSE's strict rules is an important layer of their protection plan.

The LSE has good reasons to make this market work. This is its major initiative of 2002, and after the cool reception given to Exchange Traded Funds it needs a success. The exchange's chief executive, Clara Furse, has been under a certain amount of political pressure to regain market share and to diversify into derivatives following a failed bid for the London International Financial Futures Exchange (LIFFE) in autumn 2001. The plan seems now to be to seed organic growth, and the covered warrants initiative is the largest and highest profile attempt to date to lead the LSE to new pastures – and in this case to compete with LIFFE to boot.

13. Provision of Information and Education

Covered warrants come with a publicity caravan. When launching their new covered warrants in Canada early in 2002, David Escoffier, a director at SG Cowen in New York, and Global Head of SG's Structured Products & Warrants for the Americas, said "our motto at SG is 'The SGWarrants are more than an innovative product, they are a service.'" Whilst allowing for some professional flannel, he had a point. SG committed to provide investors and investment advisers with educational materials, seminars, and a free hotline as well as access to their global SGWarrant web site for quotes, information, news, statistics and an opportunity to provide feedback.

Historically, warrant investors could have only hoped in vain for such provision. Contending with a limited flow of information was all part of the process of investing in warrants, because there was very little incentive for companies to promote their warrants. In some small way it might be beneficial for a company or trust to have its warrants in the hands of enthusiastic investors, but no extra money was to be made from explaining the merits of the warrants. As long as the share price was above the exercise price at the time of final maturity, the company would get its exercise money regardless of whether it had promoted its warrants or not. This is why companies and investment trusts have generally made no effort at all to inform warrant investors: there has been no incentive for them to do so.

On occasions this has led to extraordinary oversights. Luminar is a London-listed company which has turned in an exemplary performance, and which has used warrants in a highly innovative and laudable way to reward its employees. Its desire to have the success of the warrants, planned to mature in 2009, linked to the performance of the company meant that the warrants had a unique 'performance condition': the company's pre-tax earnings per share needed to grow at an annual compound rate of 20% for three financial years ending on 28th February 2002, otherwise the warrants would lapse. The day of the crucial results announcement came, and warrant holders waited anxiously for the text of the statement, particularly as pre-tax earnings per share was not a published figure. And there was not a word about the warrants. Then the company held a conference for analysts. Still no word on the warrants. Only when enquiries were made to the company did it respond to say that the performance condition had been met. This was very welcome news, something to crow about, but the company cannot have seen any benefit in even informing the market.

Another example of the lack of information relates to the warrant exercise notices sent out by investment trusts. These have by and large made no effort whatsoever to explain that holders would lose money by exercising the warrants at an intermediate exercise date when the warrants commanded substantial premiums in the market, or even when the shares were trading below the exercise price. Investors have frequently exercised rights when they could have bought the underlying shares more cheaply in the market, perhaps misled by these official notices with unhelpful wording. Merrill Lynch European Investment Trust, for example, announced on 5th August 2002 that just over 160,000 warrants had been exercised the previous week, gaining just 17p of intrinsic value when the warrants could have been sold in the market for 27.5p each. Again, trusts have no financial interest in providing a clear explanation of the terms; cynics point out that they benefit from small enhancements to net asset value when holders mistakenly exercise out-of-the-money warrants.

For covered warrants the economics of the issues are entirely different. The issuers make their money from margin built in to the premiums and dealing spreads, and if the market fails to thrive then it fails commercially. They have every incentive to support the market and to ensure that investors understand it, enjoy their trading, make good profits, tell their friends, and come back for more. Issuers do not have a contrary or opposing relationship to investors at all: it is not the case that if investors lose, the issuer wins. This is not a zero-sum game. The issuers' exposure to underlying assets is covered so that they are outcome-neutral (unless they choose not to be). They win commercially if demand and dealing volumes are high, which they will not achieve by investors losing money. There is no way the markets in other European countries could have thrived if this were the case.

This is why issuers are eager to promote the market with advertising, articles, guides, seminars, web sites, and other promotions to attract investors. And because there is an advertising spend to be collected, magazines and newspapers which have never previously demonstrated any interest in warrants are now clamouring to provide coverage. All market participants, whether they are issuers, brokers, publishers, or advisers, are also conscious of the fragile reputation and status of any new market, and aware therefore of the need to promote it responsibly. For this reason educational initiatives are at the forefront of all efforts, which is greatly to the benefit of investors. There is a fairly direct relationship between understanding and success. Unless they are lucky, and of course luck tends to run out after a while, investors who have little grasp of what warrants are all about are unlikely to make good profits. It is when investors with a scant understanding of warrants plough into the market that horrendous losses can be made. The wrong warrants are bought (often well out-of-the-money warrants with little chance of ever achieving value) with the inevitable result that some of them fall to zero. The ignorant investor has no idea why this has happened, blames the warrants, and vows never to touch them again. More intelligent investors can easily learn enough to feel much more comfortable with covered warrants as an investment.

The key is to understand why you have bought a particular covered warrant, what the upside and downside potential is, and at what point you might wish to sell. Some investments will still go wrong of course – no-one has a flawless record – but if you know why this has happened and understand the risk then it is much easier to accept the loss and to move on to the next investment which might make up for it. To reach this point it is not necessary to understand every intricacy of the instrument and the market: a good grasp of the basic concepts will suffice.

One huge advantage of the new market is that it will be served by some very sophisticated data providers. Historically, investors interested in warrants in the UK have been forced to puzzle over formulae whilst searching for the right functions on scientific calculators. Those with more time on their hands built spreadsheets to take the strain, but still had to input prices manually and continuously tinker with the data as warrants were issued or reached maturity. This will quickly become an impossible task for the new market if the levels of issuance typical elsewhere are reproduced. Imagine the data input required for hundreds of new warrants each month, all with non-standard terms. Imagine then setting up calculations for a range of variables including the delta and volatility. The good news is that others will do this for you and provide the information free of charge in a user-friendly way over the internet. Sites such as www.onvista.co.uk and www.warrantstats.com have been working on their systems ahead of the market opening, and should have facilities in place for investors to use from the very beginning.

Sites are being developed all of the time, so any comment is bound to become out of date, but for now one really nice feature to be found on some sites is a warrant simulator which allows users to change certain variables and to see in real-time how these might affect warrant prices. One excellent site is www.oddowarrants.fr, covering the French warrants market. A similar gadget is also available on www.citiwarrants.com. Investors can select an underlying asset which is of interest – for example, call warrants on the Italian company Mediaset, which has a current price of EU7.24. The system finds 15 warrants, but which one should a bullish investor buy?

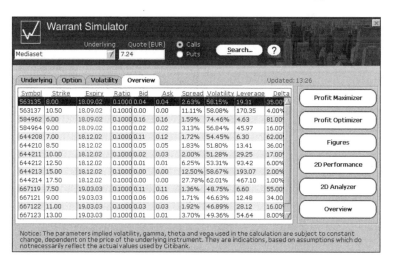

Fig 7.3 - Citibank Warrant Simulator for Mediaset warrants

Help is at hand. The '2D Performance' simulator has all 15 warrants listed and will work out their theoretical percentage gains or losses from three variables which you can adjust using sliding bars. If, for example, an investor expects the Mediaset share price to rise to rise to EU8.50 over the next 30 days, without any change in volatility, then the first warrants on the list, the 563135 18/09/02 EU8 calls, provide the best profit of 109%.

PerformanceAnalysis Mediaset				_ □ ☒

current price of underlying 7.24EUR   (?)

Symbol	Strike	Expiry	Performance
563135	8.00	55	+109%
563137	10.50	55	+13%
584962	6.00	55	+60%
584964	9.00	55	+93%
644208	7.00	146	+66%
644210	8.50	146	+85%
644211	10.00	146	+101%
644212	12.50	146	+84%
644213	15.00	146	+52%
644214	17.50	146	+33%
667119	7.50	237	+64%
667121	9.00	237	+81%
667122	11.00	237	+95%
667123	13.00	237	+100%
667124	15.00	237	+94%

	TargetPrice	8.50	
	in X days	30	
	change of volat	0.0	%

Fig 7.4 - Citibank 2D Performance Simulator for Mediaset warrants

Then the investor has second thoughts. What if this was a little too optimistic, and it takes a bit longer for Mediaset shares to reach EU8.50, say 45 days? The return on the 563135 18/09/02 EU8 calls is still good, but it has now been surpassed by other longer-dated warrants which lose less time value, and the 667123 19/03/03 EU11 calls are the most profitable with a gain of 78%.

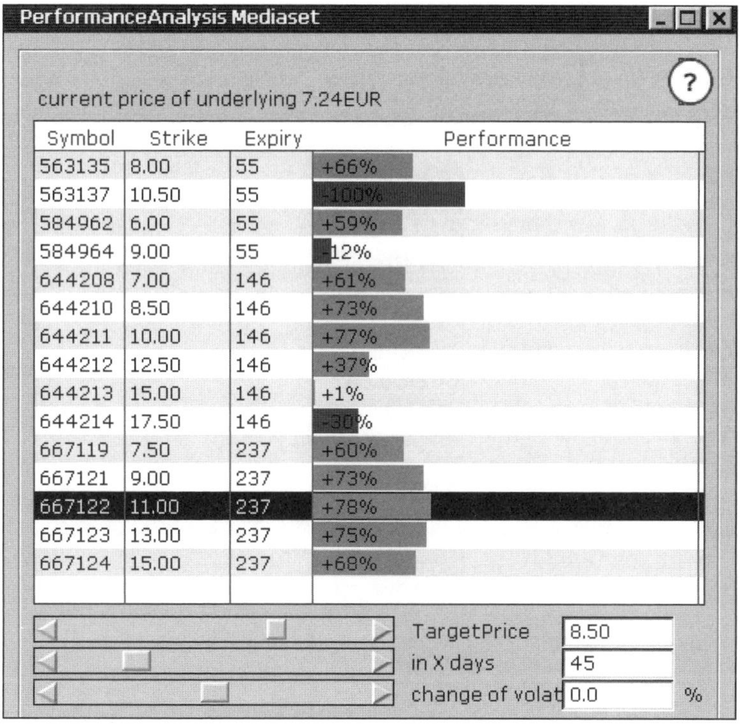

PerformanceAnalysis Mediaset ⬜ _ □ ✕

current price of underlying 7.24EUR   (?)

Symbol	Strike	Expiry	Performance
563135	8.00	55	+66%
563137	10.50	55	-100%
584962	6.00	55	+59%
584964	9.00	55	-12%
644208	7.00	146	+61%
644210	8.50	146	+73%
644211	10.00	146	+77%
644212	12.50	146	+37%
644213	15.00	146	+1%
644214	17.50	146	-30%
667119	7.50	237	+60%
667121	9.00	237	+73%
667122	11.00	237	+78%
667123	13.00	237	+75%
667124	15.00	237	+68%

TargetPrice | 8.50 |
in X days | 45 |
change of volat | 0.0 | %

Fig 7.5 - Citibank 2D Performance Simulator for Mediaset warrants

The process can be repeated for an endless stream of 'what if' questions, and users can simply drag the sliders up and down to watch the percentage price changes react. This is a superb aide for selecting warrants and also ensuring that the risk is understood – it is very easy to see what happens if price movements do not go to plan. Staying with the same example, if Mediaset shares fall to EU7.00 in 45 days' time, the short-dated warrants will lose 93% of their value – a swingeing loss – whilst the longer-dated warrants will lose 49% of value.

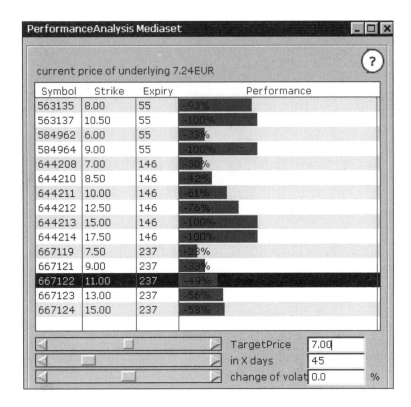

Fig 7.6 - Citibank 2D Performance Simulator for Mediaset warrants

On balance, and given that the 667123 19/03/03 EU11 calls would still provide a return of 95% if the investor's original expectations were met, he might conclude that these were on balance a better choice than the 563135 18/09/02 EU8 calls which were originally selected.

If that were not sufficiently useful, the information can also be displayed graphically, with the addition of historic performance data for the warrant price. Examining the 667123 19/03/03 EU11 calls further, the user calls up the '2D Analyzer' which features the same sliding scales, but with the forecast return shown on a graph:

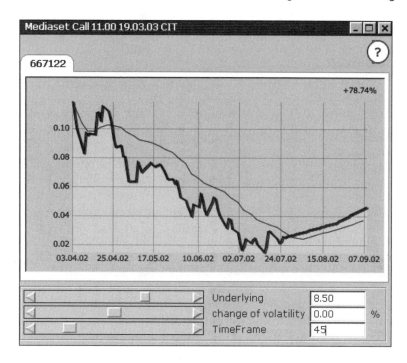

Fig 7.7 - Citibank 2D Analyzer for Mediaset warrants

Using tools such as these there is little excuse for being caught out by the risk. It is possible to consider a wide range of different scenarios – including the most pessimistic – to estimate the returns, positive or negative, which might result. Of course the simulators can only estimate, and only provide a snapshot of possible events based on current variables, but used in combination with other forms of analysis and some common sense, these facilities allow investors to be well informed as to the full scope of risks and potential rewards.

Disadvantages of Covered Warrants

1. Complexity

You need your brain switched on when dealing in covered warrants – or to delegate the brainwork to someone else. They are not as simple as shares, or even as traditional warrants, and they can get confusing at times. When you buy a share you are buying a slice of a company, which is an easy concept to understand. Derivatives are less straightforward, deriving their value from another instrument and therefore being one extra step away from the profits, assets, and true value of a company. Warrants are rights to buy or sell something, which is less tangible than buying or selling it directly: there is an extra layer of financial engineering on top, which is why they have been described as being nearer the Stock Exchange floor than the shop floor.

If you have read some guides, and this book, and just don't feel able to grasp the fundamentals of warrant investing, then the best thing to do is to walk away. You should not invest in anything you do not understand, no matter how attractive it might seem on the surface. There may be hidden dangers and unexposed risks, and it cannot be wise to be cavalier with your cash. If, on the other hand, you have a decent grasp of what is involved, then it is worth a little application to learn more. This will enhance your entire investing experience, from enjoying the whole process of selection to feeling more confident in what you are doing.

2. Adverse Price Movements

Warrants will not generally whip the shirt off your back quite as quickly as a casino croupier, but as geared instruments they have the capacity for very quick and dramatic price movements which can easily catch you out if they go the wrong way. Price elasticity works in both directions, and adverse price movements can be swift and savage. The worst five performances by stock warrants, for example, on the EUWAX market in May 2002 bear this out:

Issuer	Stock		Exercise	Date	Currency	Price 2/5/02	Price 31/5/02	% Change
ML	SAP	Call	170	7/19/02	EUR	0.21	0.01	-97.62
CENT	Muenchener R.	Call	325	9/16/02	EUR	0.35	0.01	-97.14
SOG	EMC	Call	15	9/6/02	USD	0.18	0.01	-96.11
BNP	Safeguard Scien.	Call	5	9/20/02	USD	0.13	0.01	-95.38
LB	AdvancePCS	Call	45	12/18/02	USD	0.21	0.01	-95.24

A small change in the price of an underlying asset, or perhaps no change at all, can lead to a substantial decline in the value of covered warrants. Market timing can be very important, and if you get it wrong then the results can quickly become painful. Warrants are by no means buy-and-forget instruments. When things go wrong the performance can turn very nasty very quickly, and the result can be a total loss of the money invested. Large losses can easily occur within a day, an hour, or just a few minutes, especially where the warrant is highly geared, short-dated, and based on a highly volatile underlying asset. It is important not to gloss over this aspect of warrants, which is why the whole of Chapter 10 is devoted to the subject of risk.

3. Premium

There is a price to pay for the many advantages which covered warrants confer, and that price is the premium. This is the extra amount in the warrant price beyond the value which it would have if it were to be exercised immediately, and the premiums can on occasions be very high. In particular, the premiums on covered warrants may well be higher than on UK listed equity warrants, which offer some exceptional value as they have moved out of favour. Generally, the higher premiums, higher gearing, and shorter times to maturity make it even more imperative in the covered warrants market to get it right.

4. Limited Life

One stockmarket maxim which brings a wry smile to the mouths of most experienced investors is 'a long-term investment is a short-term investment gone wrong.' Many investors have a few stale long-term holdings in their portfolios which were once-great ideas which did not quite work out. With shares, unless the company actually goes bust, there is always the option to hold for the long-term and to hope for the best. Because covered warrants have a finite defined life, this possibility is removed. In many cases warrants will be issued with a life of just one year, and at the end of that year, the warrant will expire, either with some intrinsic value, or no value at all. Covered warrants generally start with a life of between three months and three years, and never the decade-long stretches offered by some traditional investment trust warrants. For this reason covered warrants are often approached with a trading mentality, and many investors enjoy the cut-and-thrust of regular dealing which is made possible by the excellent liquidity and dealing spreads. For long-term investors though, individual covered warrants are generally unsuitable as they do not offer much in the way of longevity.

5. Time Value Decay

This is as important as it is inexorable. In the words of the poet WB Yeats, "the innocent and the beautiful have no enemy but time." He might also have included warrant investors (some of whom may also be innocent and beautiful), for whom time is no friend. Premium, or time value, disappears as warrants approach their final expiry date, which means that if the underlying asset stands still, the associated warrants will fall in value, whether they are calls or puts. Dull markets are not welcome. This in-built requirement for the underlying asset to move in the right direction is a drawback, as is the slow drip of the time value disappearing.

Time value decay, which is measured by the theta, is non-linear and will tend to accelerate as warrants near maturity:

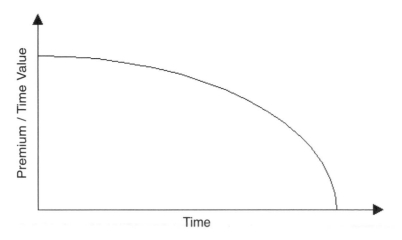

Fig 7.8 - Time value decay

As a rough rule of thumb, warrants lose one-third of their time value during the first half of their lives, and two-thirds during the second half. The accelerating loss of time value near expiry means that it is important to be aware of expiry dates and to keep a close eye on any warrants in your portfolio which are nearing their final dates.

6. Absence of Price Anomalies

Traders in the traditional equity warrants market can sometimes enjoy the fact that the market is small, overlooked, and illiquid. These features mean that price movements are far from uniform and that anomalies frequently arise. Traditional warrant prices can be very 'sticky', meaning that they do not move as quickly as their underlying shares. Frequently in the past there have been significant lags between a share moving up and the warrant following suit – creating a window of opportunity for the eagle-eyed. Where warrants are illiquid, market-makers may wait for signs of actual trading activity before moving the price, whereas an underlying share price might simply be marked higher or lower along with the market.

The pricing system for covered warrants, where supply and demand are less important factors, means that anomalies, price dislocations, and stickiness will seldom arise. This is a pity in some respects, but it should be noted that the price anomalies in the equity warrant market only arise because of the illiquidity, which can be a high price to pay. Even when price discrepancies are identified it is not always possible for investors to take full advantage, because dealing spreads can be very wide and the market size very small.

Furthermore, spotting mispricing is not always profitable even if it is possible to deal: it is not always the warrant price which moves to re-align the two securities. An apparent divergence in performance can just as easily be corrected by a fall in the share price as by a rise in the warrant price, so this approach in no way absolves investors from the need to make a sound underlying judgement.

7. No Income

Normal trading warrants do not rank for any income. They do not qualify for dividends paid on underlying shares, which in the case of higher yielding assets can be a considerable drawback. Most covered warrants are pure capital instruments, although this is not true for some of the 'investment' variants which have been developed, such as instalment warrants in Australia.

If you do require income from your securities investments then you will need to consider what proportion of your portfolio might be allocated to warrants, if any.

8. Scope Still Limited

It is all very well to suggest that covered warrants provide for a far broader coverage than traditional warrants, but their scope is still limited. Even when there might be, say, 1000 warrants listed on an exchange, a considerable proportion of these will be duplicates as far as the underlying asset is concerned. There might be 100 warrants on the FTSE 100 Index and 20 on Vodafone, but there will not be any on small AIM companies. Whole sectors of the market might not be covered, particularly when considering smaller capitalisation assets. The need for issuers to cover their exposure from a warrant issue means that the underlying instrument needs to be of a certain size and liquidity, and smaller companies do not reach the mark. You are unlikely to be able to obtain geared exposure to a small penny stock you have seen tipped in the press.

This does mean there is a danger of missing out on some good opportunities when restricting investments to the warrants universe, but in practice very few investors will invest exclusively in warrants. More commonly, warrants might form a small part of a diversified portfolio which already has a broad scope.

This is not a case against using warrants where they are available. Moreover, few investors will have the time or resources to achieve a full knowledge of entire global asset markets, or even just the UK stockmarket. A deep understanding of a comparatively focused group of companies or assets with covered warrants is probably preferable to trying to over-reach and select from what is a huge universe of potential investments.

9. No Benefit to, or Direct Link with, Companies

When a covered warrant reaches the end of its life, no new shares are issued. Even if the warrant is settled for stock, these shares will come from the secondary market. This means that there is no benefit to the underlying companies, who have no financial interest in the issue. Unlike equity warrants, the underlying company, whether it is Vodafone, Manchester United, or Amazon, does not receive any cash, which means that investors are not contributing to the health or the capital-raising requirements of the company at all by buying a covered warrant. Indeed it could be argued that covered warrants are mildly detrimental to the companies concerned because covered warrant issues can deflect investor attention away from direct investment in the shares. This has a ring of truth, but there is a counter-argument that covered warrants attract additional publicity for companies, raising their profile with investors who may later or separately invest directly in the equity. Furthermore, it is not as though covered warrants are drawing investors away from the companies' own equity warrant issues which serve a more useful cash-raising purpose. British companies have largely shunned warrants as a corporate instrument, and in very few (if any) cases will investors have to choose between an equity warrant and a covered warrant.

Another allegation is that the hedging procedures of issuers can lead to short-term market distortions. It has frequently been reported in some overseas markets that certain stocks have risen before a new covered warrant issue, because the issuer has been in the market buying stock in anticipation of a need to cover the position. This second criticism is perhaps not valid in the UK, and indeed in other European markets, where warrants are released into the market according to demand, without any minimum pre-placing requirement. Issuers can use dynamic hedging which is more subtle and less likely to cause any market disruption.

It would be stretching credulity to argue that investors feel any sense of duty, or even a sense of altruism, when investing in a company's equity warrants. Investment is usually a cold commercial arrangement, and indeed literature on trading makes much of how investors should seek to rid themselves of any emotional attachment to their holdings. If this is right, then the status of covered warrants as purely synthetic instruments, created solely for the purpose of making money from the markets, should perhaps be celebrated as something positive.

10. No Shareholders' Rights

The value of a warrant may be based on a company's shares, but as covered warrant holders are not linked directly to that company, they rank for none of the rights which shareholders enjoy. Covered warrant holders have no voting rights, will not receive annual or interim reports, and will not qualify for any shareholders' perks which may be on offer.

11. Need to Have Internet Access

Covered warrants are a new instrument, designed for the new millennium. They are also complex, which means there is a need to disseminate a lot of information – not just the price. It is difficult to perceive how this could be done through traditional print media, and the issuers are certainly set up to deliver a range of services and information electronically. Unless policies change, daily prices will not be published in the Financial Times or in other daily newspapers, although there may be some partial listings in weekly magazines such as Shares. Some guides, listings, and directories may not appear in physical paper versions at all, except where individuals have used their inkjet home printers. A considerable bulk of information will be on the internet, and the internet only. This is partly a practical matter – just consider the amount of space required otherwise to provide a decent amount of information on the new issues. On a busy day in Germany 200 new warrants can be issued, all with detailed term sheets.

If you do not have internet access, or at least access to e-mail, you may be at a considerable disadvantage. It will not preclude you from participating in the new market by any means, but there might be a constant nagging doubt as to whether you are really as informed as you could be.

Even if you are able to find complete listings of prices, do not forget that they will be out of date by the time you read them, and historic information can quickly lose value when prices are volatile and highly geared warrants are moving substantially. When dealing with high-risk securities it pays to be up to date, and of course technological advances have been extremely helpful in improving access to information for private investors. It is debatable whether there will ever be a truly level playing field for all, but the internet has succeeded in pushing a great big roller over what was previously a very bumpy surface indeed. Just six years ago advisers were still directing investors towards such sources as the microfiche in the local library, premium rate telephone services, or expensive dedicated terminals, whereas now you need merely to sit in the comfort of your own home or office and tap a few keys on your computer keyboard. This is a tremendous example of technology working to improve the lot of the private investor, at a low cost, and it would seem short-sighted not to take advantage of it. This potential disadvantage of covered warrants is easily overcome.

12. Capital Gains Tax

The taxation position of covered warrants appears on both sides of this chapter. The absence of stamp duty is an advantage over shares, but the imposition of capital gains tax (CGT) is a disadvantage when covered warrants are compared with one of their closest rivals: spread-betting.

Covered warrants, as securities, will be treated by the Inland Revenue in the same way as shares as far as CGT is concerned. This means that investors need to keep a record of all trading, and if their net gains at the end of the tax year to 5th April are in excess of the annual exemption, currently £7700, then capital gains tax will need to be paid on the excess at the investor's highest marginal rate. The rate of CGT you will have to pay depends on the level of your income liable to income tax. The amount chargeable to CGT is added on to the top of your income liable to income tax and is charged to CGT at the appropriate rates. For the tax year 2002/03, the rates are 10%, 22% and 40%. If you become liable to pay CGT, you must report your gains to your tax office.

For very successful warrant traders this could prove a significant cost, particularly as the limited life of warrants makes it difficult to manage the timing of profits to handle the tax burden efficiently. With a large and successful portfolio of shares an investor may decide to take profits on a certain proportion each year to utilise the CGT allowance, but this will not generally be possible with a portfolio of covered warrants with short maturities which mean that profits must be realised more regularly.

Similarly, it is possible in the listed equity warrants market to defer a CGT event on a very successful trade by continuing to hold the warrants until maturity and then exercising them into the shares. No CGT liability is calculated until those shares are sold, and in the meantime the holder can benefit from taper relief for long-term holdings. For short-dated, cash-settled warrants this door is closed.

Paperwork can also be a burden. You must keep all contract notes and details of your deals, and then make all of the relevant calculations at the end of the tax year, which could be a long and complicated process for frequent traders.

Whilst all investors may fear CGT and worry about their fantastic success being dented by the taxman, in reality few investors pay CGT. CGT is a relatively small tax, yielding about £1.5bn-£3bn annually for the Treasury, depending on whether it was a good year or not. Between 100,000 and 200,000 individuals pay CGT each year, and not all of those are related to stockmarket dealings.

Take CGT into account, by all means, but do not let it prevent you from investing in warrants, at least not until you have crossed the exemption limit. And every cloud has a silver lining. At least any losses incurred during warrant trading can be used to offset gains made elsewhere, or rolled forward to be used against future profits.

To finish off the subject of tax, individual warrants do not at present qualify for inclusion in an ISA, although an authorised warrant fund may be eligible.

13. Credit Risk

When you buy a covered warrant, you are doing so on the understanding that the issuer will honour its terms and provide the relevant payout at the end of its term. The issuer is your market counterparty. There is a (seemingly very small) risk of an issuer defaulting and failing to keep up its end of the deal. Whilst this is unlikely to occur, given the regulatory requirements for the financial strength of the banks authorised to issue warrants, investors have learned never to say never.

8. Analysis of Covered Warrants (i) Getting Started

Don't abandon all common sense once you have the whiff of speculation in your nostrils. You should always know exactly what you are buying, how it is valued, and what the potential profits or losses might be. All this needs is a basic understanding of some basic terms and concepts which will enable some of the principal calculations to be made. These allow for a simple comparison between competing warrants, and help to avoid expensive mistakes by steering you towards those warrants with better risk/reward ratios and prospects for capital growth.

Fundamental Analysis

Before buying any warrant you need to take a view on the likely direction of an underlying asset. Although there are several influences which have a bearing on warrant prices, the movement of the underlying asset is usually the most powerful. If you believe the asset will rise in value then you might wish to buy a call warrant; and if you believe the asset will fall in value then a put warrant may be appropriate. This is sometimes rather grandly called a 'directional strategy'. In making this judgement you may consider a wide range of factors which are largely beyond the scope of this book but which are extensively addressed elsewhere.

If the underlying instrument is a share then you may need to gauge the health of the company, its profitability, its stockmarket rating, sectoral prospects, large shareholdings, net asset value, management ability, new and existing products, competition, directors' dealings, brokers' forecasts, dividend payments, the share price chart, and possibly a whole host of other features related specifically to the company in question. Perhaps just one key driver will exert an overriding influence on the share price in the short-term.

There are a large number of books which cover this subject, plus more timely material provided by newspapers, magazines, television, on-line services, and by advisers and stockbrokers. Information and advice to assist with individual stock selection is plentiful – perhaps too plentiful – so investors relying on third-party analysis or advice may be as well to find a few trusted sources to help.

Most importantly, fundamental analysis needs to reach a conclusion on whether an asset price is likely to go up, down, or sideways, but this is not really enough. If the analysis points to a rising share price, for example, it is possible there may a wide range of call warrants to serve this purpose. But is it better buy a short-dated, highly-geared, out-of-the-money warrant or a more conservative medium-term warrant with modest gearing and some intrinsic value? Do you invest a lot or a little? To answer these questions requires some deeper thought and some more detailed steps to develop a clearer expectation for the future movement of the asset price. The judgement might be broken down into four parameters – direction, degree of confidence, size of movement, and likely time-frame.

Direction

Whilst most effort is usually devoted to trying to find assets which are likely to rise in value, with covered warrants it is possible to prosper equally from a fall in value or even a sideways movement. This has an interesting implication for the way in which investors with plenty of interest but less time might concentrate their research. Other things being equal, it can be worth covered warrant investors specialising in a particular niche, sector, or market. One drawback with this approach in the past has been that localised knowledge can seem useless for periods when the asset is not performing well. Spare a thought for Japanese and technology fund managers whose career paths happen to have directed them into areas which are massively out of favour. The merit of being able to buy call and put warrants is that views can be backed at all times, and not just occasionally when the forecast direction happens to be up.

Degree of confidence

Conclusions are not always reached with equal force. On some occasions, analysis might find a number of conflicting indicators which lead to nothing stronger than a hunch or a vague feeling that an asset could head off in one direction or another. On other occasions, a number of indicators might all point towards an outcome which can be backed with a high level of conviction. It is very useful to measure the degree of confidence you might have in any judgement because this can materially affect the selection of the most appropriate warrants. A low degree of confidence might lead you towards in-the-money warrants with modest gearing levels, whilst a more confident prediction can be backed by more volatile warrants which are perhaps out-of-the-money and highly geared so that an aggressive position can be taken.

Size of movement

Similar comments apply to the size of movement expected. If your analysis can quantify this so that you can reach a definite expectation, then your warrant choice can be tailored more effectively to maximise returns. Investors expecting a small movement in an asset which might generate a satisfactory rather than enormous profit will not want to take too much risk, so an in-the-money warrant with moderate gearing might be suitable. Clearly, however, an investor expecting an unusually large move in an asset will make the most money, if they are right, using an out-of-the-money warrant with high gearing.

Likely time-frame

Having decided which way an asset is likely to move, how confident you feel in your judgement, and what size the move is likely to be, the final question is over what period the movement is likely to occur. Whilst a long-dated warrant provides maximum leeway and opportunity for a move to occur, greater profits will be generated by shorter-dated warrants if the move happens quickly. Again, the more closely this judgement is defined, the more fine-tuned the process of warrant selection and purchase can be.

Only by answering all of these, admittedly tough, questions can you realistically choose the best warrant to support your view. If you cannot provide answers to these parameters then you are at best selecting a warrant based on a partial judgement.

Chart Analysis

Chart analysis, or technical analysis, lends itself quite well to the study of covered warrants. Many investors are looking for short-term opportunities in the warrants market, perhaps even day-trading, and charts can be of considerable help in identifying market resistance levels and turning points, finding overbought or oversold stocks, following momentum, plotting trendlines, setting target prices, and generally in timing buying and selling decisions.

Chart analysis seems particularly good at providing definite answers to vexing questions which might otherwise lead to procrastination, and although its precision can be spurious, it can be a real aid to investors who might otherwise find it difficult to make decisions, including the hard one about when to sell.

There is a large store of literature on the subject of charting which you should investigate if this line of research is of interest to you. Whether it is the use of moving averages, MACD, Bollinger bands, or Japanese candlestick charts, there are plenty of books and software packages to help. It is worth mentioning just a couple of specific points relating to warrant analysis. First of all, tempting though it might be to plot individual graphs for warrants in which you are interested, it will normally be of more use and greater relevance to stick with the underlying asset. The performance of the underlying asset is usually the most important driver of the warrant price, and it is unusual for the warrant price to move independently of the asset. Rather than potentially clouding the picture with the extra volatility, potentially thin trading, and potential data errors of covered warrants, the more easily available graphs of stocks or indices are the ones on which to focus.

Double-axis graphs

One alternative to sticking with ordinary graphs on ordinary assets and then applying the results to potential warrant trades is to plot double-axis graphs. These plot both the underlying asset price and the covered warrant price over time, on the same graph, but with separate axes so the two may be compared directly. This is a fairly primitive approach, but it enables a number of features to be seen easily and is a useful way of absorbing a lot of data in one quick glance. Double axis graphs can help you to understand:

- The history of the asset and warrant
- Trading ranges and bands
- The relationship between the asset and warrant prices
- Volatility
- Any pricing anomalies
- The decay of the time value

On the facing page is a double-axis graph of DaimlerChrysler shares and a series of Deutsche Bank covered warrants on the stock.

From the graph the generally close relationship between the two securities is apparent, as is the decay of time value from the warrants. Although this is now seen with hindsight, the break of the upwards-sloping trading band at the end of May 2002 can also be identified, suggesting a major breakout – in this case downwards.

Having applied fundamental and chart analysis to form a judgement on an underlying asset, the next step is to look for suitable warrants.

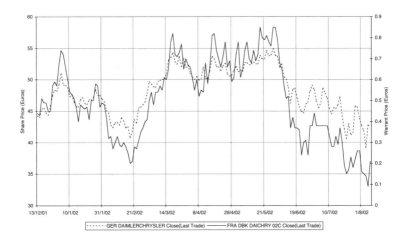

Fig 8.1 - DaimlerChrysler shares and warrants, December 2001-August 2002

Homework – Prices and Terms

This is an important section in any warrants book – indeed any book on any derivative instrument.

Derivatives derive their value from a right linked to an underlying financial parameter or security, and unless you know specifically what that right is, you cannot hope to value the derivative. That sounds so obvious, so simple, yet gullible investors regularly sail into completely unchartered waters without so much as a cursory glance at the warrant terms. Doing your homework is crucial.

It is also important to note that covered warrant terms are not highly standardised. Unlike traditional UK investment trust warrants, for example, where the bulk of the issues are exercisable at 100p, there is no such commonality in the covered warrants market. It is best to assume nothing and check everything.

The basic information for any warrant is to be found in the term sheet which is published at the time of issue, or you can generally obtain this material from a list on the issuer's web site.

The key information you need will generally fall into ten elements:

- The underlying asset
- The name of the issuer
- The expiry style (American or European)
- Type of warrant (call or put)
- Sub-type and terms for exotic warrants
- Strike or exercise price
- Cover ratio (eg 1:1 or 10:1)
- Final exercise date
- Extra information about how final price is calculated (close, last trade etc)
- Cash or stock exercise

This may seem like a lot to remember, but the information will usually be grouped together and easy to digest. You need these vital facts to value and assess warrants correctly: investing blindly without knowledge of these key parameters is unwise to say the least. Researching warrant terms is the minimum 'due diligence' work which needs to be undertaken before you invest. This is also the information you need to move on to elementary warrants analysis.

Gearing

Traditional equity investors may not be familiar with the term gearing, even though they have probably used it to make a large financial commitment. The majority of UK adults have. If you have a mortgage on a home, and perhaps a second property as well, then you have geared exposure to the UK property market. For an initial deposit of perhaps £10,000, or perhaps nothing at all, you were able to borrow the rest – for a price – and thereby gain access, and the financial exposure, to an asset worth far more.

Example

Investor buys house worth £100,000

Pays deposit of £10,000; mortgage for £90,000

House prices rise by 20%. House worth £120,000

Investor sells for £20,000 profit

After costs of mortgage (£5000), is left with profit of £15,000

Initial deposit has risen from £10,000 to £25,000 for a gain of 150%

In this instance a 20% rise in property prices turned into a 150% cash gain for the investor, who gained control over a valuable £100,000 asset for just £10,000 plus mortgage costs. This is gearing. In the warrants market, gearing is calculated very simply by dividing the asset price by the effective warrant price (ie the warrant price multiplied by the cover ratio):

$$\text{Gearing} = \frac{\text{asset price}}{(\text{warrant price} * \text{cover ratio})}$$

Example

Share price 100p; warrants 25p; cover ratio 1

$$\text{Gearing} = \frac{100p}{(25p \times 1)}$$

Gearing = 4 times

Although gearing is frequently explained and illustrated in terms of the larger profits which it can generate, it is important to note that this simple gearing calculation measures the amount of additional exposure gained by investing in the warrant, and is not a multiple for the percentage price movement. In other words, a warrant with four times gearing will not necessarily move four times as much as the underlying asset. This would only be the case if the premium were zero; otherwise the declining premium will eat into the actual leverage. This concept is explained in the next chapter. Watch out because gearing, leverage, and elasticity are all used in different ways in different markets. Check the glossary for the definitions used here.

Intrinsic Value

A warrant price is always composed of two elements, the intrinsic value and the premium.

Warrant price = intrinsic value + premium

Intrinsic value is usually the first stop for any new investor because it is the most obvious measure of value. It is sometimes called 'true' value. Even the least informed investor can see that a warrant carrying the right to buy one share at 100p will have a value of 50p if that share is trading at 150p. This is the intrinsic value: the value which a warrant would have if it were to be exercised immediately, so that:

For call warrants

Intrinsic value = asset price - exercise price

For put warrants which confer the right to sell, the equation is reversed, since the intrinsic value comes from the asset price trading below the exercise price. A warrant carrying the right to sell one share at 100p will have an intrinsic value of 30p if the shares are trading at 70p.

For put warrants

Intrinsic value = exercise price - asset price

These equations assume that one warrant carries the right to buy one share, which is not always the case for covered warrants. The equations are developed thus:

For call warrants

$$\text{Intrinsic value} = \frac{\text{asset price - exercise price}}{\text{cover ratio}}$$

For put warrants

$$\text{Intrinsic value} = \frac{\text{exercise price - asset price}}{\text{cover ratio}}$$

Intrinsic value grows along with the asset price once the asset price is over the exercise price. The chart opposite depicts this relationaship graphically.

If a warrant has positive intrinsic value, it is said to be 'in-the-money'. A warrant with zero intrinsic value, where the asset price is equal to the exercise price, is 'at-the-money'. A warrant with negative intrinsic value is 'out-of-the-money'. The degree of 'moneyness' is called the parity ratio. A call warrant exercisable at 100p into an underlying share with a current price of 110p would have a parity ratio of 1.1, or 110%.

104

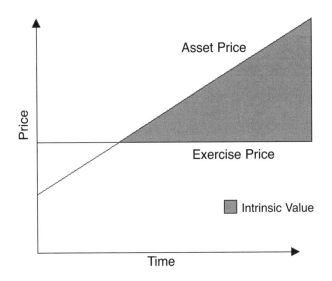

Fig 8.2 - Graphical representation of intrinsic value

For call warrants

$$\text{Parity ratio} = \frac{\text{asset price}}{\text{exercise price}}$$

For put warrants

$$\text{Parity ratio} = \frac{\text{exercise price}}{\text{asset price}}$$

To confuse matters the term parity ratio is used in some markets like the cover ratio: to denote the number of warrants required to exercise into one share. With all warrant terms it is wise to check the definitions of the terms being used before relying on data provided by a third party. The global nature of the warrants market does sometimes mean that terminology is imported from other markets where the meaning differs.

New warrants can be issued either in, out, or at the money. Sometimes a series of warrants will be issued with all variations. The fact that intrinsic value is a function purely of the share price and the exercise price, ignoring the actual warrant price, provides a clue that it is an incomplete measure of value. The second component of the warrant price – the premium – is usually more important for analytical purposes, and intrinsic value is unlikely to be a primary consideration unless you are a very cautious investor, market conditions are poor, or the warrant is close to final expiry. Intrinsic value relates to the exercise value of a warrant, so it is most relevant when a warrant is bought with the intention of holding it to full term, which is not common in the covered warrants market.

Premium

In some markets, most commonly those relating to options, the premium is the price paid for the instrument, but that is not its generally accepted meaning for UK warrants.

In the warrants market, the premium is the second element of the warrant price. In practice, warrants will not trade simply at their intrinsic value. Investors will be willing to pay extra for the benefits which warrants provide, most obviously the gearing. An asset price trading just 1% below the exercise price will offer no intrinsic value, but this does not mean that a warrant with several months of life remaining would be worthless. Investors are prepared to pay for the right to purchase the asset at a fixed price in the future, even if that price is higher than the current price.

The introduction of future expectations explains the most elementary puzzle which can confront new investors. Why would anyone want to pay for the right to buy an asset at 100p in a year's time when you can buy it today for 99p?

The answer is that the asset price may rise well above 100p in the next year, but the warrant holder will still have the right to buy it for that price, regardless of its market value.

Warrant holders will pay a premium for this right – sometimes regarded as the warrant's speculative value – and on the other side of the trading floor, issuers need to charge something extra to cover their hedging costs and to include some profit margin in the whole operation. The resulting premium is normally expressed as a percentage as follows:

For call warrants

$$\text{Premium} = \frac{(\text{warrant price} * \text{cover ratio}) + \text{exercise price} - \text{asset price}}{\text{asset price}} * 100$$

Example: asset price 80p, exercise price 100p, warrant price 2p, cover ratio 5:1

$$\text{Premium} = \frac{(2p * 5) + 100p - 80p}{80p} * 100$$

Premium = 37.50%

For put warrants

$$\text{Premium} = \frac{(\text{warrant price} * \text{cover ratio}) + \text{asset price} - \text{exercise price}}{\text{asset price}} * 100$$

Example: asset price 80p, exercise price 100p, warrant price 6p, cover ratio 5:1

$$\text{Premium} = \frac{(6p * 5) + 80p - 100p}{80p} * 100$$

Premium = 12.50%

More simply, the premium may be calculated with reference to intrinsic value as follows:

For call and put warrants

$$\text{Premium} = \frac{(\text{warrant price} - \text{intrinsic value}) * \text{cover ratio}}{\text{asset price}} * 100$$

In general, the lower the premium, the cheaper the warrant. This is because the underlying asset must rise (or fall for puts) by a percentage equal to the premium over the remaining life of the warrants for the warrants to justify their current price. The reason the asset must move by this amount is that the premium will disappear over the remaining life of the warrant. By definition the warrant is worth only its intrinsic value at expiry, which means the premium diminishes to zero as time passes. This characteristic of the premium is important, and indeed the premium is sometimes called 'time value' as a result.

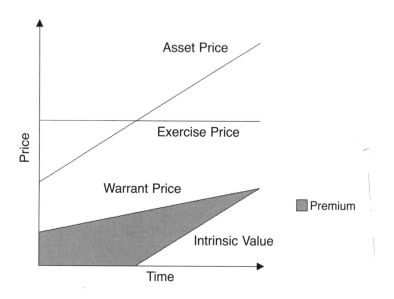

Fig 8.3 - Graphical representation of premium

Break-Even Point

In view of the diminishing premium, the asset price must usually grow for a warrant purchaser to avoid a loss. It is a simple matter to calculate the point which the underlying asset needs to reach by the maturity date of the warrants for an investment to break-even.

For call warrants

Break-even point = exercise price + (price paid * cover ratio)

For put warrants

Break–even point = exercise price - (price paid * cover ratio)

This is of limited analytical use, but the answer can be used to ensure that a purchase of warrants is consistent with your expectations of performance. A very high premium which will evaporate as the warrants reach maturity might cause the break-even point to be further away than you had realised.

The break-even point can be expressed as an annual required rate of change in the underlying asset (y=years until expiry):

For call warrants

$$\text{B/E rate} = \left[\left(\frac{\text{exercise price} + (\text{price paid} * \text{cover ratio})}{\text{asset price}} \right)^{1/y} - 1 \right] * 100$$

For put warrants

$$\text{B/E rate} = \left[\left(\frac{\text{exercise price} - (\text{price paid} * \text{cover ratio})}{\text{asset price}} \right)^{1/y} - 1 \right] * 100$$

Example

Put warrants with 2 years of life; exercise price 100p; asset price 80p; warrant price 6p; cover ratio 5:1.

$$\text{Break - even rate} = \left[\left(\frac{100p - (6p * 5)}{80} \right)^{1/2} - 1 \right] * 100$$

Break–even rate = -6.46%

Check

Year 0: asset 80p

Year 1: asset declines by 6.46% to 74.83p

Year 2: asset declines by 6.46% to 70p

Right to sell at 100p worth 30p, dividing by cover ratio of 5 = value of 6p per warrant. Warrants break even.

This annualised rate of change is useful for warrants with a life of one or two years, but is more difficult to interpret once the maturity drops to below a year. Its use might therefore be restricted on many occasions to new issues. In any event, all the figure provides is the annual rate of change in the asset for the warrants not to lose money, which is by no means a full picture.

Capital Fulcrum Point

The next step is to the capital fulcrum point (CFP), which seems to be a peculiarly British calculation. It is not generally used in overseas warrant markets. Although developed for the analysis of traditional listed warrants, it is applicable to covered warrants, and provides an extra angle from which to view their value. The beauty of the CFP is that it combines the premium and the time to expiry to provide a compound indicator allowing a fair comparison across different warrants with different maturities – and because it allows for comparison between the warrant and direct investment in the underlying it represents a significant development from the break-even rate.

The CFP measures the annual percentage change required from the underlying instrument for you to do equally well in terms of capital appreciation from the warrant. If the CFP for a call warrant is 7% and the underlying instrument grows at 8% per annum, then the warrants will outperform in capital terms. Other things being equal, the lower the CFP, the cheaper the warrant.

The formula for calculating the CFP, which is expressed as a percentage, is:

For call warrants

$$CFP = \left(\left(\frac{\text{exercise price}}{\text{asset price} - (\text{warrant price} * \text{cover ratio})} \right)^{1/y} - 1 \right) * 100\%$$

where y = years remaining.

Whilst the CFP can also be calculated for put warrants, using a slightly different formula, it does not really have any value. It would find the annual percentage fall in the asset price for you to have an equal loss on the warrant, which is not of great use. For put warrants it is better to stay with the break-even point; for call warrants the CFP is better.

Example

Call warrants with 2 years life remaining, exercise price 100p, asset price 80p, warrant price 2p, cover ratio 5:1.

$$CFP = \left(\left(\frac{100}{80 - (2 * 5)} \right)^{1/2} - 1 \right) * 100\%$$

$$CFP = \left(\left(\frac{100}{70} \right)^{1/2} - 1 \right) * 100\%$$

$$CFP = \left(1.4286^{1/2} - 1 \right) * 100\%$$

$$CFP = \left(1.1952 - 1 \right) * 100\%$$

$$CFP = 19.52\%$$

Check

Year 0: asset 80p

Year 1: rises by 19.52% to 95.62p

Year 2: rises by 19.52% to 114.29p

Overall gain in asset = (114.29p/80p) = 42.9%

$$\text{Intrinsic value of call warrant at expiry} = \frac{\text{asset price (114.29p) - exercise price (100p)}}{\text{cover ratio (5)}}$$

Value of warrant at expiry = 2.858p

Overall gain in warrant = (2.858p/2p) = 42.9%

In putting the CFP to use, its principal power is as a comparative yardstick. First, it standardises the time factor to an annual rate of growth, which allows a fair comparison between warrants with different maturities. Second, the CFP allows for comparison between a warrant and its underlying asset. An investor who has identified an attractive asset can make use of the CFP in deciding whether to invest directly in the asset, or in the warrants. If the CFP is low then the warrants may be better value, and vice versa. Third, the CFP provides a figure to be compared with investors' expectations. In deciding what constitutes a 'low' CFP expectations are paramount. As a general rule, if the CFP is below the expected annual rate of change for an asset then the warrants are likely to provide better capital returns and should be considered.

The CFP has been a mainstay of the analysis of traditional listed company and investment trust warrants for years, and it works very well when comparing warrants with, say, three years and nine years to run until expiry. It may be far less applicable however for covered warrants which are typically launched with lives between one and two years. Certainly the CFP works less well for shorter-dated warrants: it is less meaningful to use an annual growth rate when considering a warrant with three months remaining where either the break-even point in absolute price terms or the premium is more relevant. As the CFP is perhaps best used as a guide for medium-term and long-term investment decisions where value is of more importance than speculative movements, it may be an early casualty of the switch in the UK from equity warrants to covered warrants. Other forms of analysis are likely to gain more traction, so investors experienced in the equity warrants market may need to be open-minded about reducing their reliance on the CFP as a leading indicator of warrant values. Different analytical techniques likely to gain swift acceptance are explained in the next chapter.

9. Analysis of Covered Warrants (ii) Advanced

If you are not mathematically minded, you may wish to skip this section, or at least the more difficult parts of it. You can deal in covered warrants successfully without entering a labyrinth of unintelligible formulae. Advisers and information services can do the work for you, but for many investors there is a sense of satisfaction to be gained from understanding and performing the entire process of analysis. It is up to you.

Whether or not you decide to tackle the task of crunching the numbers yourself, it may still pay to skim-read this chapter to pick up the general principles behind the maths. As the issuer Citibank explains in one introductory guide, "you don't take the back off your stereo or your video recorder when you use it; you just read the instruction manual."

Black-Scholes

Formulated in 1973 by Fischer Black and Myron Scholes, and subsequently developed by Robert Merton, the Black-Scholes model has become standard usage for analysts valuing options or synthetic warrants. It is the benchmark against which all other option pricing models are compared, and it has stood the test of time.

Whether or not you believe it provides good answers is another matter, but it would be wrong to ignore it even if you doubt its efficacy: if everyone else is using it to predict prices, it will to some extent be self-fulfilling. It is the mother and father of option pricing techniques, widely used to calculate 'fair value' prices in many forms of derivative markets – not just the European-style call options for which it was first created.

The huge contribution which the Black-Scholes model has made to derivative pricing was recognised in 1997 when the Nobel Prize for economics was awarded to Myron Scholes and Robert Merson (Fischer Black died in 1995). You can count on the model being widely adopted for UK covered warrants, so at least a passing familiarity with it is useful, even if you never calculate it yourself.

The Black-Scholes formula for call warrants is as follows:

$$\text{Valuation} = a * N(d1) - \left[\left(\frac{e}{2.71828^{ry}}\right) * N(d2)\right]$$

where

$$d1 = \frac{\ln\left(\dfrac{a}{e}\right) + (r + 0.5v^2)y}{v\sqrt{y}} \qquad\qquad d2 = \frac{\ln\left(\dfrac{a}{e}\right) + (r - 0.5v^2)y}{v\sqrt{y}}$$

where   a = asset price

                 e = exercise price
                 N(d) = normal distribution function of d
                 r = risk-free rate of interest
                 y = time to expiry in years
                 v = volatility
                 ln = natural logarithm

Example

Asset price = 100p; exercise price 110p; 1.5 years remaining until expiry; volatility 40%; rate of interest 4%.

$$\text{Valuation} = 100 * N(d1) - \left[\left(\frac{110}{2.71828^{0.04*1.5}}\right) * N(d2)\right]$$

$$d1 = \frac{\ln\left(\dfrac{100}{110}\right) + \left(0.04 + \left[0.5 * 0.4^2\right]\right) * 1.5}{0.4 * \sqrt{1.5}}$$

$$d1 = \frac{-0.0953 + 0.18}{0.48989}$$

d1 = 0.1729

N (d1) = 0.5686

$$d2 = \frac{\ln\left(\frac{100}{110}\right) + (0.04 - \left[0.5 * 0.4^2\right]) * 1.5}{0.4 * \sqrt{1.5}}$$

$$d2 = \frac{-0.0953 + -0.06}{0.48989}$$

d2= -0.3170

N (d2) = 0.3756

$$\text{Valuation} = 100 * 0.5686 - \left[\left(\frac{110}{1.06184}\right) * 0.3756\right]$$

Valuation = 56.86 - 38.91

Valuation = **17.95p**

The Black-Scholes formula for put warrants is as follows:

$$\text{Valuation} = \left[\left(\frac{e}{2.71828^{ry}}\right) * N(d2)\right] - a * N(d1)$$

where d1 and d2 are the same as in the equation for call warrants, above.

Example

Asset price = 100p; exercise price 110p; 1.5 years remaining until expiry; volatility 40%; rate of interest 4%.

$$\text{Valuation} = \left[\left(\frac{110}{2.71828^{0.4*1.5}}\right) * N(d2)\right] - 100 * N(d1)$$

from calculation for call warrants, above:

d1 = 0.1729, so –d1 = -0.1729   N (d1) = 0.4314

from calculation for call warrants, above:
d2 = -0.3170, so –d2 = 0.3170   N (d2) = 0.6244

$$\text{Valuation} = \left[\left(\frac{110}{1.06184}\right) * 0.6244\right] - 100 * 0.4314$$

Valuation = 64.68 - 43.14

Valuation = **21.54p**

In this example, using an exercise price above the prevailing asset price, it makes intuitive sense that the out-of-the-money call warrant would trade at a lower price than the in-the-money put warrant. Before placing absolute faith in the results, however, it is best to remember that this is a theoretical model which is based on a range of assumptions to simplify matters. The principal assumptions are:

1. No dividends from underlying asset
2. European exercise terms (so warrants will not be exercised early)
3. Efficient markets
4. No commissions
5. Constant volatility
6. Constant interest rates
7. Returns are lognormally distributed

These basic formulae were never intended to work as catch-alls for all forms of derivatives and option-like instruments, and sure enough, the key assumptions are often violated by covered warrants. So the formula has moved on. There have been a number of adaptations, extensions, and developments of the basic Black-Scholes model over the years, such as the one by MacMillan, Stoll and Whaley to incorporate American exercise terms. Extensions have also been made to incorporate dividend payments, and it is a mistake now to think of a completely standardised formula for 'fair value' calculations. Don't scream blue murder when covered warrant issuers' determination of fair value differs from the results gleaned from the basic Black-Scholes formulae. They will probably be using subtly different models, and perhaps taking other factors into account, such as their listing, hedging and financing costs. A better approach is to regard the Black-Scholes results as an approximation and to use them to gauge whether market prices are in the same realm. If not, then some further investigation might be merited.

Volatility

Volatility is a term bandied about in the press to signify big market movements, but in the covered warrants market it has a much more precise usage which makes it of far more than descriptive importance. Two forms of volatility – historical and implied – are calculated, and widely used for valuation purposes. Historical volatility is one of the key variable inputs into the Black-Scholes equations for deriving 'fair value' prices. More volatility in an asset means more opportunity for the price to move the right way and to achieve value for overlying warrants. Investors are asked to ignore the chemical usage of the term to signify something more likely to blow up in your face. It is easy to see that a price with zero volatility – no movement at all – is no good for the majority of warrant trades, whilst huge volatility – large daily, weekly or monthly shifts in prices, can yield considerable advantages because of the 'limited loss, unlimited upside' characteristic of warrants. Yes, high volatility in the wrong direction can result in a total loss, but high volatility in the right direction can make up for it many times over.

To elaborate on this point, for the owner of a share, an increase in volatility is a mixed blessing, or perhaps not a blessing at all. The chances of the shares doing very well increase, as do the chances of the shares doing very badly. The two possibilities cancel each other out, and there is no net gain. For warrant holders, though, the equation is lopsided. The chances of the warrants doing very well is very welcome, but the chances of the warrants doing very badly is less important since the loss is limited to the price paid and unless the warrant is very deep in-the-money then the possibility of total loss on the warrant should already have been factored into the decision made. The holder benefits from the greater likelihood of really high values and is not hurt by the greater probability of really low values.

For covered warrant investors, volatility is good, a quality to be embraced. There is no need to frown next time an earnest news reporter comments on highly volatile market conditions. Too often the word is used lazily, by the media in particular, as an alternative for bad, negative, and downward, which is not necessarily what it means at all. When did you last see a headline which read 'volatile stocks post fifth straight day of large gains'? When thinking about volatility it is a good idea to think of it purely as the degree of movement.

Historical Volatility

Historical volatility measures the standard deviation of past movements in the underlying asset price. Volatility is a key input for 'fair value' analysis and for a number of other equations, so it is a useful figure to have to hand. Most of the formulae are really seeking an estimate of future volatility, but in practice the extreme difficulty of forecasting such a thing means that historical volatility is used as a proxy.

Measuring historical volatility is a simple matter of observing what has happened and making a note of the relevant prices, which many people do as a matter of course. Historical volatility figures are often provided for you by issuers on their web sites. Independently-minded investors might however like to know how these figures are calculated.

There is a standard methodology for calculating historical volatility. It is labour-intensive if the process is not automated, but for investors very keen to produce their own figures it is possible to download price data and then configure a spreadsheet to perform the calculations.

The standard volatility measure calculates annual volatility as a percentage, based on daily prices observed for a set period such as the previous 30, 90, or 250 days. The first step is to gather the data, and then to follow this procedure:

Procedure for calculating historical volatility

1. Divide the most recent price by the previous price

2. Find the natural logarithm for this number

3. Calculate the standard deviation for the range of natural logarithms

4. Multiply the answer by the square root of number of entries per year (250 for daily prices)

5. Express as a percentage

It may help to look at a real worked example, using the Adidas-Salomon share price over a 30-day period:

Date	A.S. share price	Price t/Price t-1	Natural Log
25-Jul-02	76.18	1.040426113	0.039630353
24-Jul-02	73.22	0.996190476	-0.003816799
23-Jul-02	73.5	0.992572586	-0.007455134
22-Jul-02	74.05	0.928992598	-0.073654508
19-Jul-02	79.71	1.006185307	0.006166256
18-Jul-02	79.22	1.01291395	0.012831276
17-Jul-02	78.21	1.038507502	0.037784589
16-Jul-02	75.31	1.008706134	0.008668455
15-Jul-02	74.66	0.963354839	-0.037333463
12-Jul-02	77.5	0.99871134	-0.001289491
11-Jul-02	77.6	0.980540814	-0.019651009
10-Jul-02	79.14	0.956259062	-0.044726417
9-Jul-02	82.76	0.997108434	-0.002895755
8-Jul-02	83	1.004842615	0.004830927
5-Jul-02	82.6	1.012254902	0.012180419
4-Jul-02	81.6	1.028225806	0.027834799
3-Jul-02	79.36	0.973742331	-0.026608557
2-Jul-02	81.5	0.987878788	-0.012195273
1-Jul-02	82.5	0.991586538	-0.008449054
28-Jun-02	83.2	1.015873016	0.015748357
27-Jun-02	81.9	1.004907975	0.004895971
26-Jun-02	81.5	0.970238095	-0.030213779
25-Jun-02	84	1.009615385	0.009569451
24-Jun-02	83.2	0.954237871	-0.046842298
21-Jun-02	87.19	1.03797619	0.037272847
20-Jun-02	84	1.005265677	0.005251862
19-Jun-02	83.56	1.005535499	0.005520235
18-Jun-02	83.1	0.992831541	-0.007194276
17-Jun-02	83.7	1.014176663	0.014077114
14-Jun-02	82.53	0.93890785	-0.063037941
13-Jun-02	87.9		
		Standard Deviation	0.026817338
		Multiply by square root of 250	(15.8114)
		Volatility	**42.40%**

In the Adidas-Salomon example, the historical volatility works out at 0.424, or 42.4%, which means that the normal range of share price movements is between −42.4% and +42.4% over the course of a year. Of course historical volatilities vary widely between different assets and also over time, so it is impossible to generalise about what might constitute a 'normal' range. For some guidance it is worth noting some of the current figures for major market indices and currencies, after a fairly tempestuous period. Figures for three-month and twelve-month historical volatilities, taken from the German Onvista web site at the end of July 2002, were as follows:

Index	3-month Volatility	12-month Volatility
DAX	44.27%	30.66%
Dow Jones	29.31%	22.08%
Nasdaq	48.51%	42.45%
S&P 500	30.26%	23.37%
Nikkei	29.30%	26.84%
EUR/USD	10.38%	8.83%
EUR/JPY	8.04%	9.05%

There are a couple of interesting points to note from this table.

• First, the three-month volatilities are substantially higher than the twelve-month volatility figures for all of the stockmarket indices, clearly marking out the recent period as a time of greater price movement. The longer-term context helps to make judgements about whether current volatility figures are representative and likely to continue. Care must be taken when extrapolating from historical volatility figures.

• Second, it is notable that the Nasdaq market is much more volatile than the blue-chip and broader US indices.

• Third, the volatility figures for currencies are much lower, which should caution against making assumptions about certain volatility levels being cheap. Building experience of volatility levels is a good idea to understand what is expensive, what is cheap, and to place these important figures into their proper context.

Implied Volatility

The next step is to work out the implied volatility of warrants. Implied volatility is widely used as an indicator of value. The idea is quite simple. In the Black-Scholes equations, historical volatility was one of the five inputs (along with the asset price, exercise price, time until expiry, and rate of interest) used to determine a fair value price. That fair value price can then be compared with the actual market price to form a judgement on whether the market valuation is high or low. This is useful, but labour-intensive. When considering a series of warrants, the fair value must be calculated separately for each warrant and then compared with each market price, and a percentage difference then calculated before an equal comparison can be made.

There is a simpler way, which is by using implied volatility. Instead of attempting to derive a fair value from the standard set of inputs including historical volatility, the current warrant price is substituted into the formula and the volatility omitted. It is then possible to work backwards through the equation to calculate a figure for volatility implied by the current market price. The higher the market price of the warrant, the higher the implied volatility of the asset.

Many analysts consider the assumption of constant volatility to be a prime weakness in the Black-Scholes model (volatility is itself volatile), especially as the formula is sensitive to small changes in volatility. By reorganising the formula to make volatility the unknown variable, the result provides a better measure of value. Effectively the implied volatility is the expected future volatility of the asset over the remaining life of the warrant.

Comparing Historical Volatility and Implied Volatility

The time-saving when comparing a range of different warrants on one underlying asset is that the implied volatility calculated for each warrant can then be compared with one known variable – the historic volatility. Other things being equal, the lowest implied volatility would belong to the cheapest warrant, and more generally:

- If implied volatility > historical volatility, warrant is expensive

- If implied volatility < historical volatility, warrant is cheap

In the case of the call warrants in the Black-Scholes example, where a volatility input of 40% produced a fair value price of 17.95p, an actual market price of, say, 20p, produces an implied volatility of 44.2%.

Interestingly, a data search on 145 call warrants on Adidas-Salomon shares, which had a historical volatility of 42.40%, revealed implied volatilities between 29.47% and 76.88%, so the range was very wide. The average implied volatility was 54.20%. The existence of such a wide range would suggest either that the market was extremely inefficient, or that there were other factors at play. The latter is true:

- Implied volatility is generally higher for longer-dated warrants

- Puts will often show a higher volatility than similarly structured calls

- At-the-money warrants will tend to be more expensive in volatility terms than in-the-money warrants

- Lower exercise price warrants will tend to have an implied higher volatility as well.

In other words, it would be too simple merely to be able to compare two volatilities – historical and implied – and to reach a definitive conclusion about the value of a warrant. There is no such magic wand, even though volatility comparisons are a useful tool in the analytical toolbox.

Volatility is not so important for warrants which are either well in-the-money or well out-of-the-money. Near-certainty of exercise or non-exercise means that the volatility of the underlying is far, far less important than the asset's absolute performance. For deep in-the-money warrants the vast majority of the price is made up of intrinsic value, and not premium which will vary with volatility levels. For deep out-of-the-money warrants they will have little value unless the underlying asset begins to move rapidly in the right direction, regardless of the overall volatility figure.

Volatility Smile

The lack of a direct relationship between historical and implied volatility suggests that issuers might be taking other factors into account when determining the level of implied volatility for pricing warrants. This leads to the concept of the volatility smile.

The volatility smile is a graph of the implied volatility against the exercise price, and is so called because for certain types of derivatives such as foreign exchange options, the resulting line looks like a smile. Unless you are a fan of Anne Robinson, the British television presenter known for her lopsided grin, the typical graph for share-based warrants is more of a volatility skew.

The shape of this graph has changed over time, and it is documented that, appropriately enough, the smile disappeared after the 1987 crash. This is because investors began to value deep out-of-the-money puts more highly as what academic studies by Mark Rubinstein called 'crash-phobia' took hold.

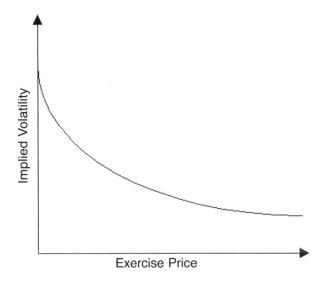

Fig 9.1 - Volatility smile

This suggests that the implied volatility used to price a warrant with a low exercise price (in-the-money for a call and out-of-the-money for a put) is higher than that used to price a warrant with a high exercise price (out-of-the-money for a call and in-the-money for a put).

Volatility Pyramid

Similarly, volatility will vary with the length of life of a warrant, and typically the greater the time remaining, the higher the implied volatility. This makes sense, since the longer the time remaining, the more opportunity the warrant has to perform: hence the higher price an investor will be willing to pay. The graph plotting implied volatility against the time to maturity is known as the volatility pyramid – not that it looks any more like a pyramid than the volatility smile looks like a smile.

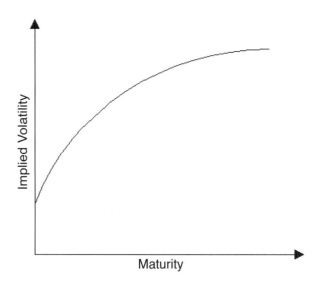

Fig 9.2 - Volatility pyramid

It is doubtful of how much practical use the smile and the pyramid can be, but the point to grasp from them is that implied volatility depends on a number of factors in addition to historical volatility, so the comparison is not straightforward. Pricing is a more intricate process.

The Greeks

When you start to look at warrants in depth, you will find numerous references to several letters of the Greek alphabet. Delta, gamma, rho, theta, and vega (actually a rogue: although Greek sounding, vega is of Spanish origin and means fertile meadowland) are all used to denote certain key parameters which can be used in warrant pricing and valuation. They are all sensitivity coefficients which allow investors to measure how the value of a warrant will be affected by a change in another variable. They have particular application when using hedging strategies. You can find much more detailed scrutiny of the Greeks, as they are known, in numerous works on futures and options, including works by the expert John Hull, but for now here is a brief explanation.

The delta is probably the most important to tackle and to understand. Delta usually refers to a rate of change, and it is no different when used in this context. It is the change expected in a covered warrant price for a given change in the underlying instrument. This is an estimate of the true gearing or leverage which will actually occur. For call warrants with a cover ratio of one the delta will always fall between 0 and 1.

$$\text{Delta range for call warrants} = \frac{0 \geq 1}{\text{cover ratio}}$$

At 0, no movement is expected in the warrants. At 1 the warrant can be expected to move penny-for-penny with the underlying asset. Typically the delta will be around 0.50 for a call warrant which is 'at the money'. The delta will move towards 0 as a warrant moves out-of-the-money, or towards 1 as the warrant moves in-the-money. This makes intuitive sense, as an example of an out-of-the-money warrant will show.

Let us assume the FTSE 100 Index stands at 4000, having fallen from 5000 over recent months. A one-year call warrant issued ten months ago has an exercise price struck at 6000, which may have been mildly optimistic at the time but looks increasingly so now. If the index needs to rise by 50% to 6000 over the next two months to achieve any value, a 50-point rise in the index is not in itself going to make much difference to the low value of the warrant. The warrant price will not move much for each point the index rises, so it will exhibit a low delta.

If for a better-placed warrant the delta is 0.5 then a penny movement in the underlying asset would imply a 0.5p movement in the warrant price. Here is an example of the delta in action:

Example

Share price = 100p.
Call warrant exercisable at 100p, price = 25p.
Delta = 0.50.
Share price moves up by 20p to 120p.
Warrant price moves by (share price change x delta) 20p x 0.5 = 10p.
New warrant price 35p.

For put warrants with a cover ratio of one the delta will always fall between 0 and −1.

$$\text{Delta range for put warrants} = \frac{0 \leq -1}{\text{cover ratio}}$$

If the delta is −0.5 then a penny movement in the underlying asset would imply a 0.5p movement in the opposite direction. Here is the same example as above, but for a put warrant:

Example

Share price = 100p.
Put warrant exercisable at 100p, price = 25p.
Delta = -0.50.
Share price moves up by 20p to 120p.
Warrant price moves by (share price change x delta) 20p x -0.5 = -10p.
New warrant price 15p.

To calculate the delta we can refer back to the Black-Scholes equation. For call warrants the delta is simply N(d1), or 0.5686 from the worked example in that section, and for put warrants it is −N(-d1), or −0.4314 from the example.

Most of the time investors will be aiming for medium-delta warrants. The received wisdom is that the comfort zone is in the range between 0.4 and 0.6. If the delta is lower than this the warrants are likely to be out-of-the-money, meaning that the underlying asset has to work hard for the warrant to achieve any value. Low delta warrants have a relatively high chance of expiring worthless, and they carry a high risk. These are the long shots which could pull off a large profit if the underlying asset moves dramatically in the right direction, but most commonly will fail. These also tend to be low-priced, 'penny' warrants which attract naïve investors like bees to a honey pot. Usually they are low-priced for a very good reason, so approach low-priced low delta warrants with caution. High delta warrants are much lower risk, but offer little in the way of gearing to make the investment worthwhile. The price will be sensitive to movements in the underlying asset, but the potential gains will not be magnified greatly. These offer a good chance of smaller profits.

Clearly the delta is a very useful indicator for assessing the likely movement of a warrant. For this alone it is valuable. It also has a second application which is equally helpful. The delta, which is sometimes expressed as a percentage for this purpose, also indicates the likelihood of a warrant finishing its life in-the-money – with intrinsic value. A call warrant with a cover in-the-money, or to restate it in more dramatic terms, an 80% chance of expiring worthless.

For call warrants

Chance of worthless expiry $= \left(1-\left(\text{delta}*\text{cover ratio}\right)\right)*100\%$

For put warrants

Chance of worthless expiry $= \left(1+\left(\text{delta}*\text{cover ratio}\right)\right)*100\%$

The delta is an extremely powerful analytical tool for interpreting the risk profile of a warrant or a portfolio. As with all statistics, though, it needs to be used intelligently. Remember that (i) the delta is constantly changing; and (ii) it provides only an estimate of the likelihood of worthless expiry, and no form of guarantee, even where the delta is 1 for a call warrant or −1 for a put.

Gamma

Richard Murphy of the Australian Stock Exchange explains gamma succinctly: "if delta is the speed of a warrant, then gamma is its acceleration." One problem with watching the delta is that it is constantly changing with the price of the underlying asset. The degree of change in the delta is measured by the gamma, which has an obvious application in dynamic models which attempt to simulate what will happen to a warrant price for different changes in the underlying asset. The gamma will tend to be greatest when warrants are at-the-money, and it will tend to be much higher for a shorter-dated warrant than for a long-dated one.

For those interested in the mathematics, the gamma is the second derivative of the change in the warrant price with respect to the change in the price of the underlying asset. It measures the convexity of the delta curve. Few investors will want to work this out for themselves, but for those who do, the formula for the gamma is:

$$\text{Gamma} = \frac{\left(\dfrac{2.71828^{-d1^2/2}}{\sqrt{2\pi}}\right)}{a*v*\sqrt{y}}$$

where d1 is derived from the Black-Scholes formula; a = asset price; v = historical annual volatility; y = years remaining.

Example

Using the same terms as for the Black-Scholes example, and taking the value of d1 from that example.

$$\text{Gamma} = \frac{\left(\dfrac{2.71828^{-0.1729^2/2}}{2.5066}\right)}{48.9898}$$

$$\text{Gamma} = \frac{\left(\dfrac{1.015056}{2.5066}\right)}{48.9898}$$

$$\text{Gamma} = \frac{0.405}{48.9898}$$

Gamma = **0.008**

What this means is that for each penny that the underlying asset rises, the delta will increase by 0.008. A 10p rise in the asset from 100p to 110p, for example, would result in the delta increasing from 0.57 to 0.65. The fact that the gamma is at its peak when the warrant is 'at-the-money' indicates that a good strategy can be to buy warrants which are slightly out-of-the-money. If they are successful and move in-the-money, the so-called 'gamma acceleration' effect kicks in to help the value of the warrants, because the delta can rise markedly in these circumstances.

Rho

The level of interest rates is unlikely to feature heavily in warrant decision-making, except perhaps in relation to the impact on the underlying asset, but for what it is worth, rho measures the sensitivity of warrant prices to changes in interest rates. To calculate rho, the formulae are:

$$Rho = \frac{e * y * 2.71828^{-ry} * N(d2)}{100}$$

where e = exercise price, y = years remaining, r = rate of interest, N(d2) is derived from the Black-Scholes formula.

Example

Warrants with exercise price of 110p, 1.5 years remaining, interest rates of 4%, N(d2) derived from the Black-Scholes formula.

$$Rho = \frac{110 * 1.5 * 2.71828^{-0.04*1.5} * 0.3756}{100}$$

$$Rho = \frac{165 * 0.942 * 0.3756}{100}$$

$$Rho = \frac{58.38}{100}$$

Rho = **0.584**

A rho of 0.584 implies that for a 1% rise in the interest rate, the price of the warrant would rise by 0.584p, and vice versa.

For put warrants

$$Rho = \frac{-e * y * 2.71828^{-ry} * N(-d2)}{100}$$

where e = exercise price, y = years remaining, r = rate of interest, N (-d2) derived from the Black-Scholes equation.

Example

$$Rho = \frac{-110 * 1.5 * 2.71828^{-0.04*1.5} * 0.6244}{100}$$

$$Rho = \frac{-165 * 0.942 * 0.6244}{100}$$

Rho = **-0.971**

A rho of -0.971 implies that for a 1% rise in the interest rate, the price of the warrant would fall by 0.971p, and vice versa.

Warrants are not generally highly sensitive to changes in interest rates. Rho is largely of interest to financial modellers working on statistical forecasts, and is often included for completeness rather than utility.

Theta

The meaning of theta can be remembered by calling it 'THE Time Attrition.' It measures the rate of decay in the value of the premium, or time value, and is usually expressed simply in terms of pence lost per day or week. A warrant losing 0.05p of time value per day will have a daily theta of 0.05. As with the other variables, the theta is not constant and will change according to the parity ratio and of course the time remaining. The theta will tend to be higher for short-dated warrants.

The convoluted formulae for calculating the theta are as follows:

For call warrants

$$Theta = \frac{\left(\dfrac{-a * \left(\dfrac{2.71828^{-d1^2/2}}{\sqrt{2\pi}} \right) * v}{2\sqrt{y}} \right) - \left(r * \dfrac{e}{2.71828^{ry}} * N(d2) \right)}{365}$$

where a = asset price; d1 and N(d2) derived from the Black-Scholes formula; y = years remaining; e = exercise price; r = rate of interest; v = historical volatility.

Asset price = 100p; exercise price = 110p; 1.5 years remaining until expiry; volatility 40%; rate of interest 4%.

$$\text{Theta} = \dfrac{\left(\dfrac{-100 * \left(\dfrac{2.71828^{-0.1729^2/2}}{2.5066} \right) * 0.4}{2.449} \right) - \left(0.04 * \dfrac{110}{1.06184} * 0.3756 \right)}{365}$$

$$\text{Theta} = \dfrac{\left(\dfrac{-16.198}{2.449} \right) - 1.556}{365}$$

$$\text{Theta} = \dfrac{-8.17}{365}$$

Theta = **-0.022**

A theta of –0.022 means that for each day that passes, the warrants can be expected to lose 0.022p of time value. Investors can decide whether to use 365 days to represent a year, or 250 for the number of trading days – the important thing is to maintain consistency.

For put warrants

$$\text{Theta} = \dfrac{\left(\dfrac{-a * \left(\dfrac{2.71828^{-d1^2/2}}{\sqrt{2\pi}} \right) * v}{2\sqrt{y}} \right) + \left(r * \dfrac{e}{2.71828^{ry}} * N(-d2) \right)}{365}$$

Example

$$\text{Theta} = \frac{\left(\dfrac{-100 \,*\, \left(\dfrac{1.015056}{2.5066} \right) *\, 0.4}{2.449} \right) + \left(0.04 \,*\, \dfrac{110}{1.06184} \,*\, 0.6244 \right)}{365}$$

$$\text{Theta} = \frac{\left(\dfrac{-16.198}{2.449} \right) + 2.587}{365}$$

Theta = **-0.011**

The theta is negative for put warrants as well as for call warrants. Both types of warrant lose time value as time passes. The theta reinforces the point that static markets are generally no use for warrant holders. Indeed the loss of time value generally accelerates as the warrant nears maturity.

The theta can also be expressed as a percentage of the warrant price, and for differing time periods – for example as a weekly percentage loss. Whilst the theta is normally a small figure, it serves as a reminder of time value decay, which adds up over time and eats into warrant values unless the underlying asset is moving in the right direction.

Vega

The final Greek is vega, which measures the sensitivity of a warrant price to changes in volatility. Vega is at its highest when a warrant is at-the-money, and tends to be higher for longer-dated warrants. The calculation is as follows:

$$\text{Vega} = \frac{a\sqrt{y} \,*\, \left(\dfrac{2.71828^{-d1^2/2}}{\sqrt{2\pi}} \right)}{100}$$

where a = asset price; y = years remaining; and d1 is derived from the Black-Scholes formula.

Asset price = 100p; exercise price = 110p; 1.5 years remaining until expiry; volatility 40%; rate of interest 4%.

$$Vega = \frac{100\sqrt{1.5} \; * \; \left(\dfrac{1.015056}{2.5066}\right)}{100}$$

$$Vega = \frac{122.47 \; * \; 0.40495}{100}$$

$$Vega = \mathbf{0.4959}$$

A vega of 0.4959 means that the warrant price would be expected to rise by 0.4959p for each 1% rise in volatility, and vice versa. The vega is usually expressed for a cover ratio of 1, but if applying the vega to a warrant with a different cover ratio it must be divided by the cover ratio first.

In some ways changes in warrant prices purely as a result of the volatility are rather analogous to investment trust shares changing in price not because the net asset value per share has changed, but because the discount or premium to net asset value has moved. This can move with you or against you, and whilst it can be irritating if volatility drops and penalises your investment, canny investors will look for reasons why the volatility of an asset might rise. This is not in itself a sufficient reason to buy a warrant, but it can lead to a 'double-whammy' gain when an asset price moves quickly, and in doing so increases volatility into the bargain.

Using the Greeks

In view of the complexity of the calculations involved in the Greeks, and the fact that the variables are truly a moving feast, changing each time the price does, you might conclude this task is not worth the effort. Fair enough. The issuers recognise both the need for investors to forecast what might happen to a warrant price for a given change in the underlying, and the difficulty of doing so. In response they frequently publish pricing matrices which indicate (they do not guarantee) what the warrant price may be for a range of under-lying prices. This information is very helpful when posing 'what if?' questions and in determining more generally whether a warrant is likely to meet your needs.

Below is an example of a price matrix provided by the Australian issuer ANZ in July 2002 for AMP call and put warrants. The stock price was A$15.65 and the call warrants were exercisable at A$18.00 by 26th September, on the basis of five warrants per share, which meant they were likely to expire worthless. Indeed the delta was only 0.0266, suggesting that the warrants would barely move in response to changes in the stock price. A one cent change in the share price should trigger a change of only 0.027 cents in the warrants; a four cent change in the shares would imply a 0.1 cent change in the warrants.

The matrix shows exactly this outcome for a four cent rise in the shares from A$15.65 to A$15.69: the warrant buying price would just rise from 2.7 cents to 2.8 cents. The puts are more interesting, being 'in the money' and with a delta of –0.2228. A one cent rise in the shares should trigger a fall of 0.22 cents in the warrants, and vice versa. A six cent change in the shares should be met by a 1.33 cent change in the warrant price. Sure enough, this is roughly the outcome according to the prices in the matrix.

AMP	AMPWAF		AMP	AMPWAR	
	American	Call		European	Call
	26-Sep-02	$18.00		24-Oct-02	$18.50
	Ratio	5:1		Ratio	4:1
$15.65	Delta	0.0266	$15.65	Delta	-0.2228
Basis	Bid	Ask	Basis	Bid	Ask
$15.51	$0.013	$0.023	$15.23	$0.830	$0.840
$15.53	$0.014	$0.024	$15.29	$0.810	$0.820
$15.55	$0.014	$0.024	$15.35	$0.800	$0.810
$15.57	$0.015	$0.025	$15.41	$0.790	$0.800
$15.59	$0.015	$0.025	$15.47	$0.770	$0.780
$15.61	$0.016	$0.026	$15.53	$0.760	$0.770
$15.63	$0.016	$0.026	$15.59	$0.750	$0.760
$15.65	$0.017	$0.027	$15.65	$0.730	$0.740
$15.67	$0.017	$0.027	$15.71	$0.720	$0.730
$15.69	$0.018	$0.028	$15.77	$0.710	$0.720
$15.71	$0.018	$0.028	$15.83	$0.690	$0.700
$15.73	$0.019	$0.029	$15.89	$0.680	$0.690
$15.75	$0.020	$0.030	$15.95	$0.670	$0.680
$15.77	$0.020	$0.030	$16.01	$0.650	$0.660
$15.79	$0.021	$0.031	$16.07	$0.640	$0.650

Fig 9.3 - ANZ price matrix for AMP warrants

Example: Black-Scholes Calculator

Input		
Asset Price	100	
Exercise Price	110	
Time to expiry (days)	547.5	
Volatility %pa	40	
Interest rate %	4	

Output	Calls	Puts
Black-Scholes Valuation	17.95	21.55
Delta	0.5686	-0.4314
Theta	-0.0218	-0.0105
Vega	0.4814	0.4814
Rho	0.5837	-0.9702
Gamma	0.0080	0.0080

Here the calculation for the call warrants is as follows where C is the change in warrant price:

$$C = \left[10p * \left(delta + \left(\frac{gamma * 10}{2}\right)\right)\right] + (theta * 14) + (vega * 1)$$

$$C = \left[10p * (0.5686 + 0.04)\right] + -0.3052 + 0.4814$$

$$C = 6.086 - 0.3052 + 0.4814$$

$$C = 6.262p \text{ (rise to 24.20p)}$$

And using the **Black-Scholes calculator** to check this outcome:

Input		
Asset Price	110	
Exercise Price	110	
Time to expiry (days)	533.5	
Volatility %pa	41	
Interest rate %	4	

Output	Calls	Puts
Black-Scholes Valuation	24.19	17.94
Delta	0.6427	0.3573
Theta	-0.0242	0.0128
Vega	0.4962	0.4962
Rho	0.6799	0.8366
Gamma	0.0068	0.0068

There is a slight difference in the figures because of course the variables are changing all the time, but this example outlines how useful the Greeks can be for forecasting warrant price changes in relation to asset price changes. That said, one final word about the Greeks is that you should resist the temptation to be swept away by the attraction of all those decimal places. Because the Greeks are constantly fluid, using them for valuation purposes can be like catching an eel in a fast-flowing river. In spite of their apparent precision they are best used for guidance and to understand risk. Typically they are used to illustrate potential profits; they are perhaps even more powerful when used to show the extent of losses when things go wrong.

Leverage

Also called elasticity and occasionally, omega, leverage measures the greater percentage movement which can be expected from a warrant price when compared with the underlying asset price. Leverage is the percentage

change ...
price. In cases where ... ,
because the leverage is the same

Example

Share price 100p; warrant price 25p; exercise price 75p; no premium
Gearing = 100p/25p = 4 times
Leverage: if shares rise by 10p to 110p, shareholder makes 10% gain
Warrants also move up by 10p in response, warrants make 40% gain
Leverage = 40%/10% = 4 times

Ordinarily, however, a premium does exist, and simple gearing will overstate the extent of leverage. This is because the premium tends to fall as the warrant gains in intrinsic value:

Example

Share price 100p; warrant price 40p; exercise price 75p; 15% premium
Gearing = 100p/40p = 2.5 times
Leverage: if shares rise by 10p to 110p, shareholder makes 10% gain
Warrants move up by 8p in response, warrants make 20% gain
Leverage = 20%/10% = 2 times

The formula for calculating leverage is:

Leverage = gearing * delta

Example

Following the example used to demonstrate the use of compound Greek indicators above, asset price = 100p; warrant price = 17.95p; delta = 0.5686.

$$\text{Leverage} = \frac{100}{17.95} * 0.5686$$

Leverage = 3.168 times

Check

For a 10p rise in the share price to 110p (+10%)

Change in warrant price = 10% * 3.168

Change in warrant price = 31.68%

Original warrant price 17.95p * 131.68% = new warrant price of 23.64p

The outcome produced by the leverage calculation is slightly lower than that reached by the Greeks, but of course the delta was rising as the asset price rose. Computing the leverage provides a tremendously powerful predictive tool which can give a quick and easy insight into the likely movement of a warrant. It can also help with calculations for certain strategies such as cash extraction. The reciprocal of the leverage tells you what proportional investment in the warrants is required to achieve the same outcome as a direct investment in the assets.

$$\text{Required investment in warrants} = \frac{1}{\text{leverage}}$$

Continuing the example above

In this case 31.566% of the investment is required to achieve the same outcome as a direct investment in the shares.

Check

£2000 investment in shares at 100p; shares rise to 110p, stake worth £2200; profit £200

£631.32 investment in warrants at 17.95p; warrants rise to 23.64p; stake worth £831.44; profit £200.12

As warrants move closer to maturity and the premium diminishes, so the leverage will tend to converge with gearing for in-the-money warrants. The corollary is that for long-dated warrants there is a considerable value in calculating leverage as well as gearing to gain a better understanding of the potential benefits and risks of investing in warrants.

Concluding Remarks

One obvious question to spring from this and the previous chapter is just how these numerous factors and forms of analysis should be combined to find the perfect warrant. Anyone advising on warrants has received the same telephone call with the plea "just tell me which warrant is the best one." The only answer to this question, which may be disappointing for those seeking Shangri-La, is that no such thing exists. There is no perfect blend. What is best for me may not be best for you. It is not being evasive to explain that different aims and risk preferences influence warrant selections in a highly individual way.

Furthermore, even if a 'best' warrant could be identified with highly attractive technical characteristics, its future price movement still depends upon a number of factors, chief among them the movement of the underlying asset. If the asset fails to move as forecast then a state of technical bliss can soon fall by the wayside as unpredictable reality barges its way through the most beautifully constructed equations. Technical analysis can skew the odds in your favour, but it cannot fix the outcome. It comes with no guarantees.

All of the mathematics in the world will not eliminate the risk, the chance of getting it all spectacularly wrong, so do not let it lure you into a false sense of security.

The sometimes unpredictable nature of highly geared covered warrants on a wide range of instruments also means that technical analysis of simple indicators such as gearing, premium, and CFP works to some degree – but less well than it does for the more homogeneous and less liquid equity warrants sector. This can be illustrated with data from the UK warrants newsletters produced over several years by The McHattie Group.

In the Warrants Alert newsletter, which has in the past covered UK listed equity warrants (although it has now expanded to incorporate the new covered warrants market), a 'Technical Merit' section is devoted to some of the warrants highlighted by its computer model as being undervalued or overvalued. This valuation is not based on a full analysis, but solely upon technical merit – the premium, time to expiry, CFP, and gearing. In the 152 months for which these tables have been published, the undervalued selections have outperformed the overvalued selections over the following month on 130 occasions. This is a success rate of 86%, demonstrating the great value of this analysis in a highly imperfect market.

A similar analysis was also undertaken for several years in the sister Covered Warrants Alert newsletter, which analysed over-the-counter covered warrants, where the undervalued selections outperformed the overvalued selections in 62 out of 89 months – a success rate of 70%. This is still an excellent outcome – any figure over 50% is good – but it does demonstrate that the use of statistical indicators for covered warrants is at best an imperfect art. Clever analysis can help you to reach investment decisions; it cannot and should not make those decisions for you.

10. Risk

No book on warrants is complete without a section on the four-letter word, risk. Ignore it at your peril. The lengthy risk warning you will encounter before you can deal through a stockbroker, and on any advisory material, is there for your benefit. It is easy with electronic communications in particular to click on the 'I Agree' button with more impatience than thought, but you should read the risk warning. It bears repetition. You should read the risk warning. Here it is. Read it now.

Securitised Derivatives

These instruments may give you a time-limited right to acquire or sell one or more types of instrument which is normally exercisable against someone other than the issuer of that investment. Or they may give you rights under a contract for differences which allow for speculation on fluctuations in the value of the property of any description or an index, such as the FTSE 100 Index. In both cases, the investment or property may be referred to as the "underlying instrument."

These instruments often involve a high degree of gearing or leverage, so that a relatively small movement in the price of the underlying investment results in a much larger movement, favourable or unfavourable, in the price of the instrument. The price of these instruments can therefore be volatile.

These instruments have a limited life, and may (unless there is some form of guaranteed return to the amount you are investing in the product) expire worthless if the underlying instrument does not perform as expected.

You should only buy this product if you are prepared to sustain a total loss of the money you have invested plus any commission or other transaction charges.

You should consider carefully whether or not this product is suitable for you in light of your circumstances and financial position, and if in any doubt please seek professional advice.

The exact wording of the risk warning may vary between firms, but the four tenets of gearing, volatility, limited life, and the possibility of total loss should always be included. The risks are real, and there is no escape from the risk/reward trade-off. One of the simplest yet most powerful graphs to be found in investment literature is a simple 45% line sloping upwards from the left, with risk and reward on either axis. The greater the potential rewards sought, the greater the risk that must be taken. There is no investment reward without risk. Even at the low end of the risk spectrum, anyone investing cash in a building society is taking a (small) risk that the building society could uncover some financial irregularity and go bust. Warrants are of course well along the risk-reward spectrum.

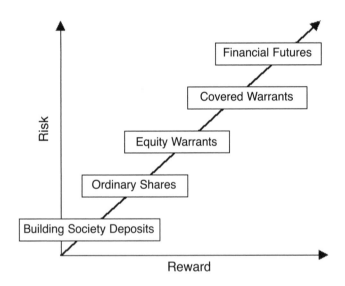

Fig 10.1 - The risk/reward spectrum

There are three reasons why covered warrants stand higher on the risk spectrum than traditional company and investment trust warrants. First, covered warrants tend to be more highly geared; second they tend to be shorter-dated; and third there is an additional layer of credit risk from the issuers as the counterparty to transactions.

A Salutary Example

Just in case you have any remaining doubts about whether warrants can really fall sharply and destroy wealth as well as create it, here is a real example of 10m Amsterdam-listed call warrants issued on British Telecom shares by Société Générale at the very end of 2000.

142

The shares at the time were trading at 654p, and the shares were issued with an exercise price of 800p, exercisable until January 10th 2003. The price of the warrants, which had a 10:1 cover ratio, was EU0.22. Since the warrants were launched, British Telecom has spun off its mmo2 subsidiary and renamed itself BT Group, and the terms of the warrants have been adjusted such that the cover ratio is now 8.98:1 and the exercise price is 718p. This does nothing at all to disguise the awful performance from the warrants.

The price of the warrants rose initially to a peak of EU0.32, a near-50% gain in the first three weeks of trading, raising hopes of telephone number profits. The prospects looked good: stockbrokers UBS rated the shares a buy, and Deutsche Bank topped that with a strong buy rating. Then it all started to go wrong. The shares and warrants both fell steadily as the TMT (telecoms, media, and technology) bubble burst, and by February 2002 when the last trade was recorded the price was EU0.02 (dealing spread EU0.01 to EU0.03). This was in effect a total loss, and no value can be expected for the warrants unless something truly dramatic happens to BT Group before January 2003. With the shares currently standing at just over a quarter of the exercise price, it does not seem likely.

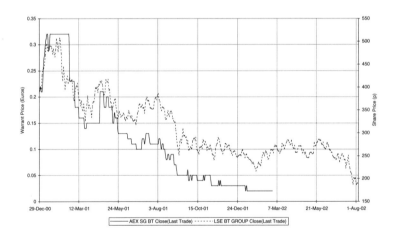

Fig 10.2 - BT Group and Société Générale BT Warrants 2000-2002

Asset price risk, amplified by leverage, is generally the main risk associated with warrants, but there are three more classes of risk to be aware of, namely takeover risk, credit risk, and currency risk.

143

Takeover Risk

For many years in the UK, warrant investors have battled with the takeover paradox. For shareholders, takeovers are nearly always welcome for short-term financial gain, as the bidder usually pays well in excess of the prevailing market price for the shares. For warrant holders though, takeovers can be a disaster because of the immediate and complete loss of time value which can wipe out the value of warrants entirely. Consider a warrant to exercise into shares at 100p, where the prevailing share price is 70p but because the shares are volatile and the warrants still have two years to run they are priced at 15p. Then a takeover is agreed at 95p, which is a good outcome for shareholders who gain 25p per share, but because the price is under the exercise level of 100p, the warrants have no value and lose their entire 15p of premium.

Covered warrants will suffer from this same potential problem, which is effectively out of issuers' hands because they cannot hedge for a takeover. Guidance provided by Goldman Sachs suggests that for a cash takeover bid or merger, the warrants will typically be cancelled and paid out at the intrinsic value. This will be calculated using the takeover bid price or the last quotation of the share before the last day of the takeover bid period. If the bid price is below the exercise price of the warrant then the investor will receive nothing. For a takeover bid or merger with a stock component, it becomes more complicated and depends on the specific details of the corporate action. Possibly the original asset underlying the warrant could be replaced with a basket representing the acquirer security and cash in accordance with the entitlement that the share would have received upon completion of the corporate event. For an entirely stock financed takeover, the underlying asset for the warrant will be replaced with the new company, and the exercise price and cover ratio adjusted appropriately to reflect the terms of the takeover. It is worth noting in this instance though that the investor does face the risk of a change in time value if the implied volatility of the target company is different to that of the acquirer (this can be advantageous or disadvantageous).

Takeovers can clearly be less of an olive branch and more of a thorny tendril on occasions for covered warrants, although much depends on the circumstances. In many cases the outcome will be positive. Overall it is doubtful whether this is likely to become a great problem for warrants on UK blue-chip companies, where their sheer size means that cash offers are rare. It is an issue to bear in mind though, and you should be careful about buying out-of-the-money warrants if part of your reasoning is based on some expectation of a takeover.

Credit Risk

If coping with specific warrant risk were not enough, there's more. In view of the stringent London Stock Exchange requirements for the financial standing of issuers, and the high levels of disclosure required, it seems unlikely that an issuer of a covered warrant would default, but this is a potential credit risk.

Investors should never say never, and the validity of accounting methods has come under much sharper scrutiny following scandals at companies such as Enron and WorldCom. The risk of issuing warrants and the decision to hedge or partly hedge the resulting exposure is all managed by the individual issuer. If you have any doubts about the financial strength of a warrant issuer, you should not buy their warrants.

Prescribed financial information about the issuer is required in the listing particulars for covered warrants, including a summary of the issuer's main activities, a profit and loss account, balance sheet, cash flow, notes to the accounts, an auditor's report, and general information on the trend of the group's business since the end of the financial year.

Currency Risk

It may be that the covered warrants market in the UK will bring a number of overseas shares and indices into the investable realm for private investors. An international flavour to the market is welcome, since it broadens choice and allows for additional diversification, but it does bring currency risk along with it. It is possible that currency movements could wipe out potential gains on a warrant, so again this is a question you should try to address – or at least be aware of – before investing.

Managing Risk

It is important to remember that there is a risk of total loss when investing in a warrant. You should not invest with money you cannot afford to lose, no matter how supremely confident you might be at the outset.

It is not wise to borrow money to invest in warrants. Unexpected events can have instant financial ramifications, and even the very best traders have been caught out on occasions. A sudden risk warning, a product failure, the departure of a key executive, a change of fashion, an accounting scandal, a political upheaval, an earthquake, or a terrorist attack could easily upset the best-laid plans.

Ways to reduce risk

There are a number of sensible steps which can be taken to reduce risk:

1. Always check the price and terms before dealing

2. Invest a sensible amount

3. Monitor prices regularly

4. Consider using stop-losses

1. Always check the price and terms before dealing

Always invest with your eyes open. Picking up a recommendation from a newsletter, for example, on a Saturday morning, and then leaving an open order to buy the warrants first thing on Monday morning, is not really a good idea. The warrants, or their underlying asset, could have changed dramatically in price by that point. Of course your work or personal circumstances may not allow you the time or access to check prices, but you should make every effort to do so if it is possible. If you are dealing through an execution-only stockbroker then you will usually receive a price quote before dealing in any event, and a good advisory stockbroker should go one step better by alerting you to any sharp movements. Staying informed at the purchase point and thereafter is a good way to manage risk.

2. Invest a sensible amount

Trawling through tips and advice from the great and the good in a book such as the Global Investor Book of Investing Rules can be more confusing than consistent, but persistence pays off when a few common threads become apparent. One oft-repeated piece of wisdom is not to invest too much in one go. Putting your eggs in one basket is widely regarded as a path to eventual ruin, even if you have some successes along the way. Sooner or later, the argument runs, disaster will strike because no investor – at least no investor telling the truth – can boast a 100% record. When you do lose, and you will, let it be a modest amount which you can afford. The trick is to invest steadily over time and to have a portfolio of holdings which can prosper through sound analysis and selection, being quite able to cope with the occasional bad apple.

The minimum amount you can sensibly invest is largely dictated by the costs of dealing, which make very small trades uneconomic in terms of the profit which must be generated just to break even. Using an execution-only

146

stockbroker who may charge as little as £10 brings the economic minimum down to perhaps £300-£400. Covered warrants do of course boast characteristics which can make them especially suitable for small-scale investment, since the gearing effect can generate meaningful profits from small sums.

3. Monitor prices regularly

If you can, try and check the prices of your warrants regularly. If it is not possible for you to check live prices during the day, then try to check up on them in the morning or evening. Covered warrant prices may move far more rapidly than many investors expect, so the moment to take profits or losses might arrive more quickly than anticipated.

4. Consider using stop-losses

Stop-loss systems have some strong advocates, such as the experienced investment writer Michael Walters, and they make very good sense in principle. The idea is to run your winners and cut your losses, specifying in advance a fixed percentage loss limit which is treated as an automatic sell signal if breached. If you buy a warrant at 100p and specify a stop-loss of 20%, then should the warrants slip to 80p, you sell without further question.

Stop-losses overcome the psychological difficulty of admitting mistakes and waiting for a bounce which never comes. It theory they remove some of the emotion from trading. Stop-losses can also be 'trailing', which means they are adjusted as prices rise. If the warrants rise from 100p to 130p, for example, the stop-loss can be moved up accordingly to, say, 110p, protecting a small profit. In this way stop-losses can become stop-profits.

Unfortunately, stop-loss limits are not always easy to administer. For covered warrants, stop-losses need to be fairly wide because of the daily volatility of prices, and this of course limits their efficacy to some extent. There is also the matter of discrete market movements. Prices often open in the morning some distance from their previous close, particularly if assets are influenced by the US or Far Eastern markets, and this can mean that prices jump straight past stop-loss limits, rendering them less effective as a loss-limitation device.

Finally, unless you are very lucky you will not find a stockbroker to monitor stop-loss levels for you, so this is something you will need to undertake yourself. This can be time-intensive if you hold a number of warrants.

Measuring Risk

It is possible to quantify risk so that it can be properly identified along with the position of a warrant on the risk spectrum. The level of risk is positively correlated with gearing, volatility, and the break-even rate, and inversely correlated with the parity ratio. A compound indicator can be built, such that:

$$\text{Risk} = \left(w * \frac{1}{\text{parity ratio}} \right) + \left(x * \text{gearing} \right) + \left(y * \text{historical volatility} \right) + (z * \text{B/E})$$

where w,x,y, and z are constants, and B/E is the break-even rate.

An overall risk factor can be calculated from a weighted formula which takes into account these technical characteristics of the warrants. This may be helpful, if imperfect. The weighting factors chosen will be arbitrary, and no account is taken either of the risk of the underlying asset, other than that expressed by volatility, but a makeshift measurement is better than no measurement at all. This would be very much a bespoke measure, but there is also one standard measure which is helpful.

Value at Risk

There is a clever calculation which can be used to measure, with 95% confidence, the maximum percentage of value likely to be gained or lost as the result of a single day's price movement. Assuming the number of trading days per year is 250, the value at risk calculation is as follows:

$$\text{Value at risk} = \frac{\text{volatility}}{\sqrt{250}} * 2 * \text{leverage} * 100\%$$

Example

Warrant on underlying asset with volatility of 40%, leverage 5 times.

$$\text{Value at risk} = \frac{0.40}{15.811} * 2 * 5 * 100\%$$

$$\text{Value at risk} = 0.0253 * 2 * 5 * 100\%$$

With 95% confidence, maximum percentage gain or loss likely in a single trading day = **25.3%**.

The results from this equation can be eye-opening: some of the prospective price movements are very high. There is some debate over whether the correct number of days to use for this equation is 250, the approximate number of trading days per year, or whether holidays and weekends should be included to make it up to 365. In practice it is most important that calculations are performed consistently, so that the same number of days is used to calculate both the volatility and the value at risk. The value at risk equation can of course be modified for different time periods. To find, for example, the maximum percentage of value likely to be gained or lost in a month, simply replace 250 with 12 in the equation. It does, however, become less useful as time periods are extended, and the results must sometimes be adapted because the maximum loss cannot exceed 100%.

Taking Responsibility

When dealing with any risk, it is important to take responsibility. Hiding with your head in the sand is a bad approach. Blaming the market is a bad approach. Blaming market-makers or the issuers is a bad approach. Losing sleep because you are worrying about the risks is a bad approach. Recognising the risks, weighing them, choosing to accept them, managing them, and then accepting the outcome is an altogether healthier and more satisfying way to invest, meaning that you can enjoy the challenge – and hopefully the profits – without any sleepless nights.

The way in which you invest, and the covered warrants which you consider the right ones for your investment approach, will depend on your own profile and preferences. Investing is a personal matter, which is why there is such a wide range of financial products competing for attention in a diverse market-place. It is impossible to generalise about how much of your portfolio and your wealth you might invest in warrants. They are a high-risk instrument, but for some investors that is acceptable. There are some basic guidelines which might help:

1. What is my expertise?
2. What is my risk preference?
3. What is my overall investment position?

This first point is worth devoting some thought to, and answering honestly. Newcomers to the market should start modestly, and invest more later, or use riskier strategies once some experience and some profits have been amassed. The second point will depend upon your personality and circumstances. Typically, younger investors tend to be prepared to take more risks with their capital because they are earning more to replenish any losses, because they are ambitious for gains, more optimistic, and because their financial responsibilities may be limited. Or you may have put aside a pot of speculative money which you are happy to risk, and to have some fun with along the way. This leads on to the third point, about your overall investment position. If warrant trading is central to your wealth then you may well wish to consider some lower-risk tactics to build overall value, whereas a generally conservative investor who has earmarked, say, 2% of a large investment portfolio for purely speculative purposes can afford to be more aggressive. This is an individual matter, as is the responsibility for your investment decisions.

Advice

You need not be entirely alone, however. If you are unsure of the risks you are taking, you should take professional advice before investing. This need not be an admission of failure, or a cry for help, but simply a recognition that others with a different perspective, and perhaps more time and resources, can help you to maximise your investment opportunities. An intellectual partnership with an adviser, where they produce a stream of ideas from which you can pick and choose, can be both satisfying and profitable. Most importantly, an adviser may help you to avoid costly mistakes. A dash of scepticism from time to time is no bad thing to challenge your views and analysis.

The London Stock Exchange will not be able to give you advice on individual warrants, and nor will issuers. There will be very few independent advisers or stockbrokers with much expertise on warrants when the market is launched, since it is new to most of them too, but some educational efforts will be directed specifically at this professional group, and it is to be hoped that some will develop a deep interest. It has been suggested that asking a potential adviser to explain the Greeks will soon sort the wheat from the chaff.

11. Strategies

Given the variety of warrants available, the range of different benefits, and the array of analytical approaches, it is hardly surprising that there are a number of different ways you can play the game. It has been known for larger investors to order special warrants bespoke, and certainly in markets with a diverse range of covered warrants available it is possible to tailor your holdings and trading approach neatly to fit your individual requirements. For every reader of this book there will be different preferences, thoughts, and ideas. It would be an impossible task to explain all of the trading techniques which you might employ. You can enjoy discovering and learning these as you participate in the market and receive help and advice along the way. Generally though, covered warrants are not instruments for long-term investment. They are tools with which you can pursue specific investment strategies. Without exploring this topic in a comprehensive way, it is worth a look at three main strategic categories – speculation, hedging, and cash extraction.

Speculation

Warrants are most commonly branded as highly geared financial casino chips, or white-knuckle roller-coaster rides for investors with strong stomachs. This may or may not be fair, but let's not forget that casinos and roller-coasters can be great fun. People flock to them for entertainment and an adrenalin rush. If the experience in other overseas markets is replicated, and it probably will be, then the bulk of activity in UK covered warrants will be short-term trading by investors seeking to make quick profits. One major issuer in France said that a surprisingly high proportion of trading in its warrants consisted of day trading, and that the average holding period for its warrants was around two weeks. Narrow dealing spreads, the absence of stamp duty, and the ability to deal through cheap execution-only stockbrokers mean that the costs of getting in and out quickly can be very low, and of course market volatility has been providing plenty of openings for the brave and fleet of foot. Traders have a chance of success in these conditions: whether they capitalise on the opportunities depends on their own guile, methodology, and judgement.

Using covered warrants for speculative purposes means taking advantage of their gearing in an aggressive way. Instead of buying 1000 shares for £1000, you may find a five-times geared warrant to provide exposure to 5000 shares for the same investment. This accentuates the potential gains (and losses).

Traders will usually be looking for high historical volatility, deltas and leverage, and probably a short time until expiry. Warrants with these characteristics offer plenty of potential for action, although this comes with a commensurately high risk. And at the risk of repeating the point, the speculative gains can be staggering. Consider this excerpt from the June 2002 issue of In the Money, a monthly newsletter published by SG Australia, outlining the performance of a warrant on Rupert Murdoch's News Corporation with a cover ratio of four and the trading code NCPWGK:

> "A Lazarus-like performance by NCP has effectively delivered a 'get out of jail card' to holders of NCPWGK. With expiry rapidly approaching, this A$13.00 May'02 call was all but worthless in early May. Despite Gemstar being written down to the tune of US$2.4bn, NCP reported third quarter 2002 net profit after tax of US$235m with all divisions except newspapers posting double-digit increases. NCP shares rose from a May low of A$11.54 to trade as high as A$13.89 over the month. NCPWGK initially traded up to A$0.21 on the news, up from a month low of A$0.019 (that's not a typo). NCPWGK has since settled back to A$0.14 (basis A$13.45)."

Shareholders may have been pleased with their gain from low to high of 20%, but these short-dated warrants which multiplied in value by eleven times over the same period demonstrate just how successful warrants can be on occasions. Presumably, though, these highly speculative warrants were tucked away in a dark corner of the market, and were not actually traded by Australian investors at the time? Wrong. The NCPWGK warrants were the second most active of all SG Australia warrants from 1st May to 19th May 2002, with 6.35m warrants traded. This is a real example, and real profits were made. Just to complete the story though, the last price on the warrants before their expiry was A$0.069, showing just how important it was to trade these warrants actively to extract a good profit. In this short period these warrants encapsulate much of what investors need to know about the risks and rewards of speculative warrants.

To some degree there is a speculative vacuum in the UK market at present which covered warrants might be well placed to fill. Penny shares used to be the punters' favourite in the 1980s, then traditional investment trust warrants had their place in the sun for a couple of years in the mid-1990s before the technology boom drew in a whole new generation of speculative investors. Then, of course, it spat them out again, and the subsequent (possibly consequent) bear market caused demand to wither. This torrid experience has made investors wary of investing in smaller growth companies and has caused a swing back towards larger, sensible, value stocks with a solid base of earnings. But greed is still a factor, and many investors cannot resist the lure of something to spice up an otherwise dull portfolio. Using covered warrants to turbo-charge a small portion of your wealth is certainly an idea to consider. Deriving the extra profit potential from a transparently structured instrument offering gearing is also seen as preferable at present to moving down the asset quality scale in search of greater returns.

Hedging

For private investors, hedging is probably more of a theoretical possibility than a common usage. Most investors take a view and back it. Or if things go wrong they accept the loss. On occasions though it can make sense to hedge a portfolio, where you wish to protect it, for example, against the possibility of a market fall but do not wish to sell your holdings for tax reasons. Covered warrants can be used effectively in this role where they are available.

Delta Neutral Hedging

The delta can be used in a simple way to estimate hedging requirements. If an investor has 10,000 shares and wishes to buy the correct number of warrants to hedge the position – to cancel out any gains or losses – then the right quantity can be calculated using the delta:

$$\text{Number of warrants required} = \frac{\text{number of shares}}{\text{delta}}$$

To hedge an existing portfolio, put warrants need to be used. If a put warrant exists with a delta of 0.4, for example, the investor would need to buy (10,000/0.4) 25,000 of the warrants to create a delta neutral hedge position. If the shares were to fall in value by 50p, creating a loss on the shares of £5000, the put warrants would increase in value by 50p multiplied by the delta of 0.4, so 20p each. With 25,000 warrants the gain works out at £5000, exactly cancelling out the loss on the shares. This is easy, but it is of course an approximation. Because the delta changes, this is a fragile balance which requires periodic adjustment, or rebalancing. In the example given, the rise of the put warrants would have increased their delta, meaning that fewer warrants were now required to match the equity exposure. When operating a dynamic hedging policy such as this, an investor might consider the value of gamma for the warrants concerned, since this indicates the rate of change in the delta. A high gamma would imply a need for frequent adjustments.

Cash Extraction

In risky, nervous, unpredictable markets, the cash-extraction approach to warrants can make very good sense. It is often overlooked. Casual observers tend to focus on the more obvious and exciting trading applications without realising that warrants can be applied to a portfolio to reduce risk and to fulfil a defensive strategy. Gearing can be interpreted defensively to keep a toe in the water without getting a soaking if markets move the wrong way. Rather than gearing up and investing the same amount by buying more warrants, investors can gear down and obtain the same exposure to the underlying assets for less money, releasing the balance for other use and reducing the maximum possible loss.

The number of warrants which should be bought to maintain the same profit potential as that from a shareholding can be calculated using the same formula as used for the delta hedge, except that it now relates to call warrants:

$$\text{Number of warrants required} = \frac{\text{number of shares}}{\text{delta}}$$

This is best demonstrated with an example.

Example

Shares trading 120p; warrants exercisable at 100p trading at 30p; delta 0.8.

Investor holds 10,000 shares, worth £12,000.

Obtains same exposure by buying 12,500 warrants at 30p. Cost = £3750.

Cash extracted = (£12,000 - £3750) £8250

Check on performance

Scenario A: shares rise by 20%.

Shares rise by 24p to 144p, shareholder value £14,400. Profit = £2400

Warrants rise by 24p*0.8 = 19.2p, to 49.2p.

Value of 12,500 warrants = £6150. Profit = £2400

Scenario B: shares fall by 20%.

Shares fall by 24p to 96p, shareholder value £9.600. Loss = £2400.

Warrants fall by 24p*0.8 = 19.2p, to 10.8p.

Value of 12,500 warrants = £1350. Loss = £2400

This example demonstrates that employing the cash-extraction technique can deliver the same profits and losses, but with less capital tied up. In this case the £8250 of cash extracted can be put to work in other ways, perhaps in low-risk securities or interest-bearing accounts. And the maximum loss in the case of a calamity is reduced from £12,000 invested in the shares to £3750 invested in the warrants. Used in this way, warrants can actually reduce portfolio risk substantially.

Alas there is no foolproof way of using warrants to guarantee a better return in all circumstances, and although this defensive use of warrants has many merits, it is not without drawbacks. In addition to the lack of dividends and rights which accompany a switch from shares to warrants, there is also the matter of time value decay. There is a cost to holding the warrants, and this can mean a worse return if the underlying share falls modestly or stands still. Continuing with the example above:

Scenario C: shares unchanged; warrants lose time value

Shares 120p, shareholder value £12,000. No profit or loss

Warrants fall by 10p to intrinsic value of 20p

Value of 12,500 warrants = £2500. Loss = £1250

This strategy is good, but not perfect. Any search for a flawless methodology to enhance returns will prove fruitless, and the best approach is to find ways of using warrants which most closely match your own views and aims. If you want to delve into the possibilities further, there is a whole raft of strategies which can repackage the risk and reward characteristics in ways to suit individual needs.

Long-Shot Investing

Long-shot investing combines extreme caution with extreme risk. For some it may present the best of both worlds. If you can remember the days of cash housekeeping, this is rather like having a flutter at the bookies with whatever is left in the tin at the end of the week. Whilst the word 'guarantee' should perhaps not appear anywhere in a book about warrants, investors can use warrants defensively as part of a capital guarantee policy whereby the strategy is to keep all of your core capital safe. If you have £10,000, place it in an interest account, or in gilts, or premium bonds, or wherever you think you can get the best return whilst keeping the money safe. In this low inflation environment your interest is not of great necessity to maintain the real value of your capital, and in any event it may not amount to enough to be meaningful. On £10,000 you might achieve £450 of interest in a year at current rates. Investing that £450 in ordinary equities is unlikely to make you rich, unless you are extremely lucky, but by investing in highly geared warrants you can obtain some reasonable exposure for this small sum. Investing in warrants with 10 times gearing will provide exposure to £4500 worth of assets, providing a much better opportunity of making the size of profit which would actually make a difference. And if you lose this money, your core capital is still secure.

Straddles and Strangles

A straddle, sometimes also called a spread-eagle, is a two-warrant strategy which can pay when an asset is expected to move sharply but the direction is not known. There are plenty of circumstances where this might occur: when a gold-mining company is expected to announce some key drilling results; when a retailer reveals its Christmas trading figures; for a market generally around the time of an election; when key economic data is due; when chart analysis indicates that a range breakout is about to occur.

A good example is provided by the FTSE 100 Index, which between November 2001 and May 2002 traded in a narrow band between 5000 and 5400 points. Chart analysis showed a sideways band pattern, suggesting a long and weary battle between buyers and sellers to determine market direction. Theory suggested that when the index broke out of the band then the movement would be significant, particularly after such a long period of range trading.

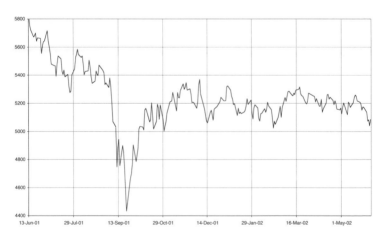

Fig 11.1 - FTSE 100 Index, June 2001-May 2002

The problem was that no direction was forecast, so buying a call warrant or a put warrant would not guarantee success if the market then set off in the other direction. The solution was a straddle – to simultaneously buy a call and a put on the index. Initially this may sound like a waste of money, since surely the two will cancel each other out? Not if the movement in the index is large enough, since the strategy takes advantage of the unlimited upside, limited downside quality of warrants to produce a profit as long as the profit on whichever warrant turns out to be the winner is greater than the overall loss taken on the other warrant.

In the event, in 2002, the market broke out of its trading range sharply – in a downward direction.

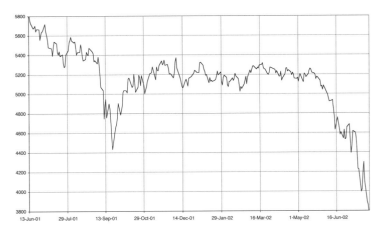

Fig 11.2 - FTSE 100 Index, June 2001-July 2002

So taking a theoretical example of how a straddle might have worked (a Black-Scholes calculator has been used to provide realistic prices):

Example

Index 5100; call warrants with exercise price of 5000 and cover ratio of 50 priced at 13p; put warrants with exercise price of 5000 and cover ratio of 50 priced at 9.5p.

Investor buys 38,000 call warrants, total cost £4940.

Investor buys 52,000 put warrants, total cost £4940.

Total investment = £9880.

Index falls to 3800 over course of two months

Price of call warrants falls to 1.3p. Value = £494. Loss = £4446

Price of put warrants rises to 24p. Value = £12,480. Profit = £7540

Net profit = (£7540-£4446) £3094

In this case the investor banks a 31% profit on the straddle even without predicting the direction of the price movement. In practice, the profit could have been even larger, since the call warrants could have been sold once the new downward trend became apparent.

The theory behind a straddle is also well represented graphically:

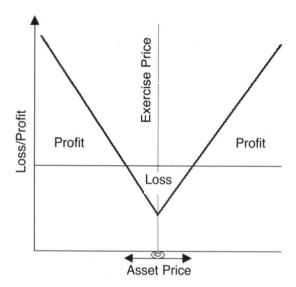

Fig 11.3 - graphic illustration of straddle

The movement to generate a sufficient profit must be significant, hence the area of loss in the centre of the graphic where the asset price has not moved much and the diminishing premiums on the warrants outweigh the net profit. Unless premiums are low it may be difficult to make this strategy work in practice. That said, the example above may understate the true profit because the premium should have been boosted by the increase in volatility. Investors considering this strategy might be wise to undertake one or two theoretical 'dry runs' first to check that the profits can exceed losses by a sufficient margin to justify the risk.

You might also come across the term 'strangle'. A strangle is like a straddle, but with different exercise prices for the calls and puts:

Example

Index 5100; call warrants with exercise price of 5500 and cover ratio of 50 priced at 9p; put warrants with exercise price of 4500 and cover ratio of 50 priced at 5p

Investor buys 55,000 call warrants, total cost £4950

Investor buys 100,000 put warrants, total cost £5000

Total investment = £9950

Index falls to 3800 over course of two months

Price of call warrants falls to 0.5p. Value = £275. Loss = £4675

Price of put warrants rises to 15.5p. Value = £15,500. Profit = £10,500

Net profit = (£10,500-£4675) £5825

In this example the outcome was a higher profit of 59%, but the extra risk was of a total loss on both warrants if the index had stayed within the range 4500-5500. Again this can be shown graphically:

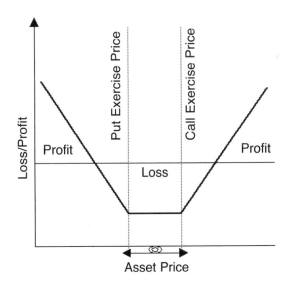

Fig 11.4 - graphic illustration of strangle

This chapter was intended as a taster to whet your appetite for covered warrants, irrespective of what type of investor you may be. It would be going too far to say that warrants offer something for everybody. They do not offer much to the poor, the completely risk-averse, or to the naïve. For the rest of us, though, they are an everyday instrument for everyman. Whether you think markets are going up or down, you can benefit by using warrants. Whether you wish to gear up your portfolio or protect its value, you can benefit by using warrants. Whether you wish to double your stake in the market or halve it, you can benefit by using warrants.

12. The Future

The covered warrants market in the UK looks set to get off to a solid if slightly pedestrian start, with plenty of prospects for expansion thereafter. After all, London has a lot of catching up to do. And there are plenty of successful market models to follow, which London could emulate with a fair wind from global stockmarkets. No-one could accuse the London Stock Exchange of introducing covered warrants at the top of the market to cash in on investor demand, as the launch comes after over three years of dismal market performance.

The poor market backdrop has unfortunately led to some severe cuts in marketing budgets which mean the start of the London covered warrants market has been reduced to a 'soft' launch with some background marketing and public relations work taking the place of a major advertising campaign. It may take a little while for the market to gain supporters and to build momentum.

It will help the market if recent global stockmarket weakness abates, values recover, and private investors again find investment in securities more of an exciting than a chastening experience. Most trading is likely to be in call warrants initially, although the flexibility of the instrument may mean in time that the industry is less cyclically vulnerable than the traditional market in call-only warrants.

A broadening and deepening of the covered warrants market can be expected once it has become established. A broadening should take place as more issuers arrive, having let others take the risk of the launch, and the number of warrants from which to choose rises accordingly. Some major global players with considerable size and market presence, such as Citibank, have pulled back from the opening of the market, but will be watching developments closely and will surely join in if trading volumes start to rise. This is good, as more issuers means more pricing competition, but for investors the 'deepening' of the market is perhaps of greater interest. Although it might not seem this way to novices, the UK market is starting by keeping things simple. The issuers and the LSE decided that more complex warrants would confuse, mislead, and eventually stifle demand as inexperienced warrant investors grappled with unfamiliar jargon and information. Most warrants will therefore be plain vanilla to begin with. More exotic and cleverly structured 'investment' style warrants can follow later once a base of education has been achieved.

The educational drive could well attract younger investors who are happier to take risks, open-minded about new products, internet-savvy and often cash-poor, which means they are attracted by the prospect of gaining decent exposure for less money up front. If the market is successful in attracting this group, then its future could be assured for some time to come. In the near-term, the media can help (or hinder) the development of the market. Historically, newspapers and magazines have provided very little coverage of warrants, writing just an occasional introductory article. It is to be hoped – if not expected – that this time the size and versatility of the market might stimulate more interest and encourage more journalists to spread the word. Already a new quarterly warrants magazine is on the blocks, and some newspapers and magazines which have never previously considered warrants to be anything other than a fringe activity are starting to pay more attention.

Whatever support may be provided though, the success of the new market ultimately rests on the provision of warrants which investors wish to trade, and are able to trade profitably. It is reasonable to be optimistic about this prospect, but not complacent. Covered warrants are effectively a brand new product in the UK. There are a few problems which could arise. The first relates to the support of the issuers, who are participating for commercial reasons and do not have bottomless pockets. If some evidence of demand for warrants fails to emerge reasonably quickly, they could depart as soon as they have arrived to concentrate on their established and lucrative European markets. Their specialist staff and information technology systems are expensive. Second, there is the very limited market capacity on the LSE's CWTS order book system, which some issuers have also complained imposes comparatively high costs. A better – and probably cheaper - system may need to be developed if the market is truly to prosper to the full extent witnessed in markets such as Germany, Italy, and Spain.

For now though the immediate prospects are tantalising. The UK looks set to have more warrants than ever before, more choice and variety, more liquidity, more instruction, more backers, and a fresh set of regulations written specifically for the protection of private investors.

The ingredients are in place: let us hope it is a recipe for success.

Sources of Further Information

Newsletters

Warrants Alert is a monthly advisory newsletter which has been published continuously since 1989. Generally, however, there is little physical material, and the bulk of relevant information is to be found on the internet.

The internet

Australian Stock Exchange	http://www.asx.com.au
Citibank	http://www.citiwarrants.com
Commerzbank	http://www.warrants.commerzbank.com
Dresdner Kleinwort Wasserstein	http://www.warrants.dresdner.com
Financial Services Authority	http://www.fsa.gov.uk
FTSE International	http://www.ftse.com
Goldman Sachs	http://www.gs.com/warrants/
JPMorgan	http://www.jpmorganinvestor.com
London Stock Exchange	http://www.londonstockexchange.com
Macquarie Bank	http://www.macquarie.com.au
McHattie Group	http://www.londonwarrants.co.uk
McHattie Investment Management	http://www.mchattie.co.uk
Oddo & Cie	http://www.oddowarrants.fr
Onvista (German site)	http://www.onvista.de
Onvista (UK site)	http://www.onvista.co.uk
Société Générale	http://www.warrants.com/uk
Trading Lab (Italian site)	http://www.tradinglab.com
UK Warrants Info	http://www.ukwarrants.info
Warrants Alert	http://www.tipsheets.co.uk
Warrants Daily	http://www.warrantsdaily.com
Warrants Magazine	http://www.warrantsmagazine.co.uk
Warrant Stats	http://www.warrantstats.com

Glossary

This list of commonly used terms relating to warrants refers wherever possible to the most common usage in the UK market. Please note that different meanings can be ascribed to some terms in other markets or by other market participants.

American-style
A warrant which can be exercised at any time until final expiry.

Ask
The buying price of a warrant.

At-the-money
The underlying asset price is equal to the exercise price.

Barrier Warrants
Warrants with an additional 'barrier' clause in the terms. Usually the warrants expire when a barrier level is breached.

Basket Warrants
Warrants over a group of securities, often within a sector.

Bid
The selling price of a warrant.

Bid-only
A bid-only warrant is 'sold-out' so that it may not be possible to buy any more.

Black-Scholes
Derivative pricing formula constructed by Fischer Black and Myron Scholes in 1973, and very widely used for 'fair value' calculations.

Break-even Rate
The annual percentage growth rate required from the underlying instrument for you to break-even (avoid a loss) on a warrant.

Calls
Call warrants give the right to buy an underlying instrument, and are normally used to back a bullish judgement.

Capital Fulcrum Point
The CFP measures the annual percentage growth rate required from the underlying instrument for you to do equally well in terms of capital appreciation from a warrant.

Cash Extraction
A defensive strategy using warrants to replace the exposure to assets at a lower price, thereby releasing cash.

Cash-settled
Cash-settled warrants may not be exercised in exchange for a physical asset, but for a cash amount equal to their intrinsic value.

Corporate Warrants
Warrants issued directly by companies or investment trusts, exercisable into their own shares. Also known as traditional or equity warrants.

Corridor Warrants
Warrants designed to pay out a fixed amount for as long as an underlying asset price trades within a specified range, or corridor.

Cover Ratio
Number of warrants required to exercise into one share, or one unit of the underlying asset. Also known as the subscription ratio, exercise ratio, conversion ratio, entitlement ratio, parity ratio, multiplier, or set. Take care when applying the cover ratio. Some issuers express the ratio as an inverse, so that a cover ratio of 100 will be written as 0.01.

CWTS
Central Warrants Trading Service, the automatic execution order book system on the London Stock Exchange.

Delta
The change expected in a covered warrant price for a given change in the underlying instrument.

European-style
A warrant which can be exercised only at the final maturity date or at other fixed times.

Exercise
When a holder decides to take up the rights given by a warrant.

Exercise Price.
The fixed price at which the warrant holder can buy or sell the underlying asset. Also known as the strike price.

Exotics
Warrants with complex exercise terms.

Expiry Date
The date stipulated by the issuer on which the holder's rights in respect of a covered warrant end.

FSA
Financial Services Authority, the regulator for UK covered warrants.

Gamma
The degree of change in the delta for a given change in the underlying asset.

Gearing
The degree of additional exposure gained by buying a warrant. Gearing is calculated by dividing the asset price by the warrant price.

Hedging
A strategy to protect the value of an asset or portfolio.

Historical Volatility
A measure of the standard deviation of past movements in an underlying asset price.

Implied Volatility
The level of volatility implied by a warrant price.

In-the-money
Positive intrinsic value: ie the underlying asset price is above (calls) or below (puts) the exercise price.

Intrinsic Value
The value which would be realised were the warrant to be exercised immediately. For calls this is the underlying asset price minus the exercise price; for puts it is the exercise price minus the underlying asset price.

Leverage
A measure of 'true gearing' which measures how much more a warrant will move in percentage terms against the underlying asset. Calculated by multiplying the delta by gearing. Also known as elasticity, or omega.

Liquidity
The ease of dealing in a warrant.

LSE
London Stock Exchange.

Offer-only
When a warrant is offer-only you cannot sell it back to the issuer.

Out-of-the-money

Negative intrinsic value: ie the underlying asset price is below (calls) or above (puts) the exercise price.

Parity Ratio

A measure of 'moneyness' or intrinsic value.

Plain Vanilla

Warrants with fairly standard exercise terms, without special clauses.

Premium

The extra amount (in excess of intrinsic value) you pay for buying a warrant. Also known as time value.

Puts

Put warrants give the right to sell an underlying instrument, and are normally used to back a bearish judgement.

Rho

A measure of the sensitivity of a warrant price to changes in interest rates.

RSP Gateway

A centralised routing system for electronic links between stockbrokers and Retail Service Providers (RSPs), who provide electronic pricing and execution services.

Securitised Derivative

A derivative which is freely traded and listed on a stock exchange.

Stock-settled

A warrant is stock-settled when it is exercisable in exchange for a physical security such as a share. Also known as physically settled.

Straddle

Call and put warrant strategy designed to benefit when a sharp price movement is expected but the direction is unknown.

Strangle

As for straddle, except that the put and call have different exercise prices.

Theta

Measures the loss of time value. Usually expressed in pence per day or per week.

Trigger Warrants

A form of warrant which triggers a one-off payout in the event of an underlying asset reaching a specified level.

Value at Risk
The maximum percentage of value likely to gained or lost as the result of normal price movement, typically over one day.

Volatility
The degree of movement in an underlying asset, measured by standard deviation. May be either historic or implied.

Vega
A measure of the sensitivity of a warrant price to changes in volatility.

VWAP
Volume Weighted Average Price used to calculate some closing prices on the London Stock Exchange.

Bibliography

Understanding Trading and Investment Warrants
Australian Stock Exchange, 2002

What is a Derivative?
Australian Stock Exchange

Connaitre les Warrants
Frédéric Bériot, Le Journal des Finances, 2001

Factbook 2002
Bolsa de Madrid

The Covered Warrant Market
Borsa Italiana, 2001

An Insight into the World of Warrants
Gizelde Brady, Jacques Schaefer and Richard Swain, SG Securities

Trading in Options
Geoffrey Chamberlain, Woodhead Faulkner, 1990

Guide des Warrants
Credit Agricole Indosuez, 2002

Call & Put Warrants on Shares and Market Indices: a Guide
Credit Lyonnais, 2000

An Introduction to the Warrant Market in Australia
Credit Suisse First Boston

Go For Warrants
Euronext, 2002

Warrants Ingeniously Transacted
EUWAX, 2001

Proposed Listing and Conduct of Business Rules for Securitised Derivatives
Financial Services Authority, 2002

Warrants on the London Stock Exchange: Pricing Biases and Investor Confusion
Gordon Gemmill and Dylan Thomas, City University Business School, London, European Finance Review 1: 31–49, 1997

Options, Futures, & Other Derivatives
    John C Hull, Prentice Hall, 2000

Global Investor Book of Investing Rules
    Philip Jenks and Stephen Eckett, Harriman House, 2001

Understanding, Trading and Investing in Warrants
    Johannesburg Stock Exchange, 2002

The Covered Warrant Market Technical Guide
    London Stock Exchange, 2002

Investor's Guide to Warrants
    Andrew McHattie, Financial Times Prentice Hall, 1996

Covered Warrants Alert
    The McHattie Group

Warrants Alert
    The McHattie Group

Equity Warrants
    Julian Redmayne, Euromoney Books

In the Money
    SG Australia

Seize the Opportunity
    SG Warrants

Trading Stock Options and Warrants
    Chris Temby, Wrightbooks, 2001

Index

Warrants Alert newsletter

A subscription to Andrew McHattie's Warrants Alert newsletter is a must for all newcomers to the market. First established in 1989, Warrants Alert has now been re-launched as an 8-page monthly newsletter for beginners and first-time covered warrants investors.

Warrants Alert offers education and specific advice on which warrants to buy and sell. The newsletter covers all forms of UK warrants in a clear and simple style, easy for novices to understand.

The only advisory newsletter available to private investors, Warrants Alert sets out to find the bargains through a combination of research and sophisticated analysis. It advises you which warrants to buy (and why) and also when to take your profits. By learning about this emerging market now you can leap one step ahead and tap into the large profits available from warrants which are selected carefully and wisely.

You may opt to receive Warrants Alert by e-mail or post. If you choose the e-mail version it should look exactly like the paper version of the newsletter and you will be able to print it out yourself. For subscription details, please visit our web sites at www.tipsheets.co.uk or www.londonwarrants.co.uk, or telephone us on 0117 925 8882.

Warrants Alert Professional

For experienced warrant investors seeking more detailed monthly information and even more advice, Warrants Alert Professional is a 16-page monthly advisory newsletter.

Warrants Alert Professional is a specialist in-depth publication and an annual subscription costs £199.

Harriman House Ltd

Andrew McHattie on Covered Warrants is published by Harriman House Ltd. Harriman House is a specialist publisher of financial books for both retail investors and for the professional finance community. To see our complete list of titles, please visit:

http://www.harriman-house.com

If you have any comments about this book, or want to make an enquiry of any kind concerning our publishing operation, please email Philip Jenks on:

books@harriman-house.com

or telephone him on +44 (0)1730 233870.

Global-Investor.com

Harriman House is part of Global-Investor.com, a company involved in financial education across a number of formats. Our main business is running the world's leading online financial bookshop:

http://www.global-investor.com

On Global-Investor.com, you can browse over 5,000 financial titles from large and small publishers, covering a wide range of subjects. We have a reputation for quick and efficient service, competitive prices, and rapid delivery.

If you would like to receive a free printed catalogue of financial books, please complete the online request form at:

http://www.global-investor.com/catalogue

or email catalogue@global-investor.com with your name and address and 'catalogue' in the subject line.